NYC
'07

Modern British Architecture since 1945

PREFACE BY
NORMAN FOSTER,
Royal Gold Medallist for Architecture 1983

EDITED BY
PETER MURRAY & STEPHEN TROMBLEY

First Published in Great Britain 1984 by Frederick Muller Limited,
55 Great Ormond Street London WC1N 3HZ in conjunction with RIBA
Magazines Limited.

© 1984 RIBA Magazines Limited

British Library cataloguing in Publication Data
I. Murray, Peter II. Trombley, Stephen
Modern British architecture since 1945.
(RIBA Guides to modern architecture)
1. Architecture, Modern – 20th Century – Great Britain
III. Series
720'.941   NA968

ISBN 0-584-40006-3

Printed and Bound in Great Britain by R. J. Acford, Chichester, Sussex

Contents

ACKNOWLEDGMENTS

The editors are grateful to Lynda Relph-Knight for her organisational skills as editorial assistant. Ingaret Eden helped with proof-reading while Alan Thompson did additional research. Jan van der Wateren and Robert Elwall of the British Architectural Library advised on the select bibliography and on photos respectively.

The following contributed entries to the *Guide*: Bill Ainsworth (Northern); Tony Aldous (London); John Baird (Northern Ireland); Jonathan Ball (South West); Alan Berman (Southern); Brian Carter (East Midlands); Tony Collier (West Midlands); Colin Davies (London); Keith Garbett (Eastern); John Henning (Wales); Keith Ingham (North West); Tom Jestico (London); Barry Russell (Southern); Sutherland Lyall (Southern); Philip McKlean (Southern); David Millard (Yorkshire); Richard Murphy (Scotland); Peter Murray (London); Hugh Pearman (London); Lynda Relph-Knight (London); Kathy Stansfield (London); Ted Stevens (South West); David Thurlow (Eastern); Stephen Trombley (London and Northern Ireland); Brian Waters (London); Sam Webb (South Eastern).

Photographs (reference is to entry numbers): Anderson + McMeekin (317, 322); Robert J. Anderson and Co. (319); James Austin (28); Cedric Barker (247); Peter Bloomfield (71); Richard Bryant (101, 142, 188); Stuart Campbell (301); Mandy Cawthorn (70); Martin Charles (29, 37, 44, 90, 100, 136, 153, 228, 243, 332); Andrew Clarke (240); Richard Davies (262); John Donat (1, 15, 25, 49, 52, 61–2, 64, 104, 116, 135, 145, 157, 191, 193–4, 197, 203, 207–8, 227, 241, 313); Richard Einzig (2, 8, 17, 18, 23–4, 34, 38, 43, 50, 66, 79, 82, 114, 126–7, 176–7, 201, 229, 235, 242, 251, 259, 277); Elsan, Mann + Cooper Ltd (164); Ezra Stoller Esto (65); Forestry Commission (265); Keith Gibson (97, 140, 146, 278–9, 284); GLC Photographic Unit (133); Bruno de Hamel (16, 206); Dona Haycraft (22); Andrew Holmes (45); Pat Hunt (109); A. L. Hunter (298–9); R. R. Inglis (314); Donald I. Innes (274); Ben Johnson (139); Winter Kidson (147); Robert Kirkman (219, 236); Ken Kirkwood (3, 106, 156, 333); John Kyle (38); Sam Lambert (31, 119); Edward Leigh (11); Leighton Gibbons Arps (266); John Maltby (26); Eric de Mare (35); Donald Mill (86); John Mills (162, 165, 172–5, 275); Tom Molland (264); Keith Murray (222); Christine Ottewill (68); Photo-Mayo Ltd (154–5, 159); Jeremy Preston (151–2); John Price (12); Tim Rawle (13, 30); John Rawson (33, 199); Jo Reid and John Peck (141, 167, 187, 244, 253); Rigmor Mydtskovt Steen Ronne (123); Barry Russell (180–1, 186, 215–16); Henk Snoek (4, 21, 73, 78, 90, 103, 158, 170, 207, 220, 248, 255, 269, 272–3, 280, 283, 287, 293–4, 300, 306, 308); Terence Soames (327, 330); Spanphoto (288, 310); Steve Stephens (271); Tim Street-Porter (92, 115, 233); Studio Brett (286); William J. Toomey (124); Stanley Travers + Partners (323, 331, 336); Morley von Sternberg (107); Hylton Warner & Co Ltd (326); Colin Westwood (27, 59, 144, 245); John Whybrow Ltd (267).

Preface

This Guide fills a long vacant gap by bridging across cities and regions to present a nation-wide picture of modern architecture that dates from the 1950s through to barely completed new works.

Although intended primarily to assist the foreign architect or student, it should also prove an invaluable source of information for anybody who is interested in architecture. The task of selection is made enjoyably easy by a clear combination of photographs, descriptions and indexed references.

If I have any personal regrets then those are concerned with a desire to see how the diverse threads of the last thirty years have their roots in earlier buildings - both mainstream and seminal — but the continuum of history is such that it always presents the dilemma of where to start. Perhaps this offers clues about a follow-up; otherwise this Guide looks like being a difficult act to follow in terms of the contemporary scene.

Norman Foster
Wiltshire
July 1983

Introduction

To produce a list of fewer than 400 buildings from the hundreds of thousands which have been constructed during the post-War era in Britain is a difficult task. The guide aims to be selective rather than comprehensive.

Buildings were chosen because they are important in the development of post-War architecture, because they are fine examples of their type, or because they are well enough known to be buildings a visitor would already have on his list. For this reason there is a bias towards more recent buildings. Earlier buildings which were thought to be important at the time of their construction were found in a number of cases to be uninteresting to the contemporary visitor.

Entries are arranged geographically according to the thirteen regions of the RIBA. Cities and towns are listed alphabetically within each region. Each entry gives details of the name of the building and its architect, its date of completion, and details of any awards it has received. Directions for getting to the buildings by public transport or by car are included, along with relevant telephone numbers and information about access.

We have not included a comprehensive selection of maps, assuming that most visitors would already be equipped with these.

Most of the entries are concerned with single buildings or single complexes of buildings. However, there are two significant areas of post-War building not covered in detail in the guide, but worthy of comment: new towns and universities.

Any visitor wishing to gain a comprehensive view of architectural progress during the period should make an effort to visit the new towns which emerged during the post-War era to accommodate the increasing population and to generate economic recovery and growth. Early new towns followed on from the 'garden city' principle established by Ebenezer Howard at the turn of the century, and first put into practice at Letchworth (1903) by Raymond Unwin. The New Towns Act of 1946 provided for eight new towns in the London region and six in other parts of Britain, though that number has grown considerably following early successes. The new towns are interesting from a social, economic and planning point of view as well as from an architectural one. Some new towns, most notably Milton Keynes, have stimulated new and exciting architectural developments, but have not been without their problems, both architectural and financial. A list of the new towns and their dates of designation is included below:

ENGLAND			
Aycliffe	designated 1947	Hemel Hempstead	1947
Basildon	1949	Milton Keynes	1967
Bracknell	1949	Northampton	1968
Central Lancashire	1970	Peterborough	1967
Corby	1950	Peterlee	1948
Crawley	1947	Redditch	1964
Harlow	1947	Runcorn	1964
Hatfield	1948	Skelmersdale	1961
		Stevenage	1946

After the new towns, the most significant architectural expansion in Britain was in the new universities built between 1960-1970. When the University of Sussex was founded in 1958, in an attempt to accommodate the 'war babies' who had now got their 'A' levels, the existing universities realised that they could not cope with the student numbers projected for the next decade. In 1959, the University Grants Committee (UGC) set up a Sub-Committee on New Universities and obtained support for a further six universities. The new universities aimed to be big by British standards, accommodating some 3,000 students each, and were required to find sites of at least 200 acres on which to build.

Sussex was planned by Sir Basil Spence, who used pink brick and segmental concrete arches to create a coherent vocabulary on a sloping site. The new university, modern in design and interdisciplinary in its educational aims, was soon as a symbol of how university education would proceed in the future.

York followed closely in 1960 as the second of England's new universities. Robert Matthew Johnson-Marshall and Partners were appointed consultant architects. The vice-chancellor wanted a collegiate system, so the central discipline was established. All but a few specialised buildings employ a modified version of the CLASP system which was versatile from a functional point of view, but resulted in an uninteresting skyline. Sir Denys Lasdun's development plan for the University of East Anglia was presented in 1962 and quickly established principles now accepted as commonplace: compactness, short walking journeys between buildings and segregation of pedestrians and vehicles.

In 1962 Lord Holford was appointed consultant architect to the University of Kent, and the University of Essex plan (by Kenneth Capon of Architects' Co-Partnership) followed in 1963. Kent adopted an intimate collegiate system on a 300 acre farmland site, while Essex opted for a series of rectangular buildings with students housed in 15-storey tower blocks. Warwick University, also on a parkland site, was initially master planned by Coventry chief architect Arthur Ling with Alan Goodman, but three other firms replaced the original team in succession. The last of the seven English universities to be approved was Lancaster in 1966. Gabriel Epstein of Shepheard Epstein planned it according to a collegiate model, and it has been praised as the new university which underwent the least growing pains. Robert Matthew Johnson-Marshall and Partners' Stirling University in Scotland was a significant contribution to the architecture of the region.

Recent government cuts in university spending ensure that further growth will not take place in the near future. The following is a list of green field universities designed between 1958 and 1968:

University	Date	Architect
Sussex	1958	Sir Basil Spence
York	1960	Robert Matthew Johnson-Marshall and Partners
East Anglia	1962	Sir Denys Lasdun
Kent	1962	Lord Holford
Essex	1963	Kenneth Capon, Architects' Co-Partnership
Warwick	1964	Arthur Ling & Alan Goodman; Yorke Rosenberg and Mardall; Renton, Howard, Wood Associates; Shepheard and Epstein
Lancaster	1966	Gabriel Epstein of Shepheard and Epstein
Stirling	1968	Robert Matthew Johnson-Marshall and Partners

HOW TO USE THIS GUIDE

The thirteen regions of the RIBA, along with Scotland, Ulster and Wales, are arranged in alphabetical order. Within each section, entries are arranged alphabetically by city or town, with individual buildings listed alphabetically under city or town headings. The following symbols are used:

🚗 directions by car
⇌ nearest British Rail station
🚌 bus to take (from BR station unless otherwise specified)
⊖ nearest London Underground station
Ⓜ nearest Tyne and Wear Metro station
☎ telephone number for further information

In London, visitors are recommended to use the *A-Z* street map or *Nicholson's Street Finder*. In Oxford and Cambridge, most booksellers stock street maps which identify university buildings. Indices listing building types, towns, names of buildings and architects are placed at the end of the book.

PETER MURRAY
STEPHEN TROMBLEY
London 1984

Eastern

Bedford
BEDFORD MIDLAND STATION, Ashburnham Road, Bedford. *British Rail Midland Region Architect's Department.* 1978.
≥ Bedford

This building largely replaces a Victorian station altered over the years. The new station includes a number of traditional elements such as glazing and exposed steel structure, but in a totally uncompromising way. The careful landscaping is particularly successful, providing a well-defined podium for the new building.

Bury St Edmunds
GREENE KING BONDED WINE AND SPIRIT STORE, Maynewater Lane, Bury St Edmunds. *Lyster, Grillet and Harding.* 1974.
Award: Structural Steel Design Award 1975.
≥ Bury St Edmunds ☎ 0284 63222

The brief for this building was simple – to provide a secure store for wines and spirits. The security aspect is reflected in the design of this elegantly detailed steel frame structure with brown steel cladding. It is of credit to the Greene King Brewery to have commissioned two fine buildings in this and the Michael Hopkins scheme (below).

Bury St Edmunds
GREENE KING BREWERY, Maynewater Lane, Bury St Edmunds, Suffolk. *Michael Hopkins Architects.* 1979.
Awards: RIBA Award 1980; Constrado Award 1980; Financial Times 1980.
≥ Bury St Edmunds ☎ 0284 63222

It is exciting to find a building designed with such control and elegance. The exposed steel structure supporting the ground floor above the flood plains of the River Linnet leads up to a simple grid of columns and steel lattice roof. Colour has been avoided in the design, enabling the activity within the building to provide visual excitement.

1

2

3

Bury St Edmunds
MATSUDANA, 8 Diomed Drive, Great Barton, Bury St Edmunds, Suffolk. *Jack Digby*. 1966.
Award: Civic Trust Commendation 1967.
🚗 off A143 ☎ 0284 87445

An example of simple, well thought out domestic architecture, this house with its nicely landscaped grounds stands out on an indifferent low density estate. Construction is a simple post and beam timber structure with whitewashed brick walls. Planned around a courtyard, the design creates the illusion of a larger house, while giving privacy.

Bury St Edmunds
HOUSING AND SOCIAL CLUB, Rushbrooke Village, Nr Bury St Edmunds, Suffolk. *Richard Llewelyn-Davies and John Weeks*. 1965.
Award: West Suffolk Bronze Medal for Architecture 1967.
🚗 Ipswich Road from Bury St Edmunds ⇌ Bury St Edmunds

Set around the village pump among mature trees, this scheme shows just how good modern domestic architecture can be. Whitewashed brickwork and solid pitched roofs give a delightfully relaxed feeling and provide a sense of community.

Subtle detailing of the windows and curves of the walls provide a counterpoint to the traditional styling.

Cambridge
ADRIAN AND BUTLER HOUSES, TRINITY COLLEGE, Grange Road, Cambridge. *David Roberts and Geoffrey Clarke*. 1978.
⇌ Cambridge ☎ Bursar 0223 358201

A series of linked pavilions, these two buildings sit comfortably in their park-like setting close to the University Library. Brick construction is combined with a wholly timber clad floor culminating in pantiled roofs, and reflecting Roberts' interest in Italian architecture. Probably the richest example of Roberts' work in Cambridge, the buildings harmonise with the varying range of large houses in this predominantly residential area.

Cambridge
AGNEW HOUSE HOSTEL, Evelyn Hospital, Trumpington Road, Cambridge. *Cambridge Design*. 1976.
Awards: RIBA Award 1976. Civic Trust Award 1978.
🚗 A10 to Trumpington Street ⇌ Cambridge ☎ Administrator 0223 353401

Though relatively small with modest painted brickwork and asbestos slates, the nursing home is rich in design and variety of detail. The two-storey L-shaped block hints at a courtyard on the entrance side. The garden side is in strong contrast, creating a domestic scale appropriate to the more private spaces. Throughout the building contrasts of brick and timber and of solid and void are exploited, sometimes to the point of awkwardness.

4

5

6

7

Cambridge

AGRICULTURAL RESEARCH COUNCIL GREVILLE BIOCHEMISTRY LAB-
ORATORY, Institute of Animal Physiology, Babraham, Cambridge. *Colin St John Wilson*. 1971.

🚌 A604 to Babraham ⇌ Cambridge ☎ 0223 832312

Following the extensive laboratory building of the 60s, this scheme benefited much from its predecessors. The planning and internal zoning as
well as the servicing arrangements are worth close examination. Architec-
turally, the building is a simple rectangle clad with Cor-Ten steel. It has
weathered well, demonstrating the great potential of the cladding material.

Cambridge

BAR HILL VILLAGE HALL, Village Green, Bar Hill, Cambridge. *Keith Garbett*. 1979.

🚌 A604 to Bar Hill ⇌ Cambridge 🚌 from Drummer Street, Cambridge

Clearly influenced by Venturi, the design for this hall in a new suburban
village boldly expresses the formal parts of the building. The scheme has
suffered from the self-help building programme which detracts a little from
its overall success. But the concept is tough enough to withstand these
shortcomings and the building will no doubt respond well to the inevitable
changes which community demands require.

Cambridge

BENSON AND MALLORY COURTS, MAGDALENE COLLEGE, Magdalene Street, Cambridge. *David Roberts*. 1952–70.

⇌ Cambridge ☎ 0223 61543

Part old, part new, the buildings around these courts represent the best
of Cambridge college and domestic buildings. With the exception of the
Lutyens Building, Roberts was involved throughout the development of
the courts working with a number of notable assistants. The existing half-
timbered and pantiled houses have been lovingly restored as residential
accommodation, with three major new buildings and a variety of smaller
additions. The complex is linked in a way that allows each project to retain
its own architectural identity while respecting its surroundings, proving
again that Roberts was a remarkable architect.

Cambridge

BOAT HOUSE FOR CORPUS CHRISTI AND SIDNEY SUSSEX COLLEGES,
Victoria Avenue, Cambridge. *David Roberts*. 1959.

⇌ Cambridge

Set on the banks of the Cam, this delightfully simple symmetrical building combines a solid lower boat storage area with a light steel-framed first
floor housing the changing and club facilities. The effect on a bright summer's day is almost that of a Mondrian painting, combining the design symmetry with the symmetry of reflection in the water. Two spiral staircases
counter-rotating at either side add a particularly nice touch.

8

9

10

11

Cambridge

CHURCHILL COLLEGE, Storey's Way, Cambridge. *Sheppard Robson.* 1968.
Award: RIBA Award 1968.
≋ Cambridge ☏ Bursar 0223 61200

The design for Churchill College was the result of a competition. It comprises a central building containing administrative offices, dining hall and JCR with routes running out to a series of residential courts. Other communal accommodation such as the chapel and library is remote from the main block. The large site includes sports grounds, a rarity for Cambridge colleges, and enables the buildings to be viewed as a group within the landscape. Very much of its time, the complex is flat roofed with Brutalist detailing.

Cambridge

CLARE HALL, Herschel Road, Cambridge. *Ralph Erskine.* 1969.
≋ Cambridge ☏ Bursar 0223 63330

This building has never gained the recognition of the RIBA or other award sponsors. Even so it is extremely successful and enjoyed by residents and visitors alike. The design includes a number of surprises and subtle details impossible to describe in this brief outline. But the combination of communal and private spaces allows families and individual students to co-exist happily, a rare achievement, and includes many Scandinavian ideas that are readily accepted.

Cambridge

CRIPPS BUILDING, St John's College, Cambridge. *Powell and Moya.* 1967.
Awards: RIBA Bronze Medal 1968. Civic Trust Award 1968.
≋ Cambridge ☏ 0223 54688

One of the most successful modern buildings in Cambridge, this residential block sits comfortably on a site running from the river's edge into the parklands adjoining Queen's Road. In an almost magical way it manages to separate the private and public functions of a college building. An analysis of the building's form and function may not satisfy the purist, but this is of little importance compared with its greater successes.

Cambridge

CRIPPS COURT, Queens' College, Silver Street, Cambridge. *Powell, Moya and Partners.* 1979.
Award: RIBA Commendation 1982.
≋ Cambridge ☏ Junior Bursar 0223 65511

Here the architects had the difficult task of relating the new block to existing buildings on either side of the river, while enabling it to assert itself. The new court manages to stand in its own right, featuring a careful and clearcut use of materials. Within the court, the residential blocks taking up three sides are perhaps over simple, while the dining room is a strange mixture of light tracery and heavily detailed roof.

12

13

14

15

Cambridge
DARWIN COLLEGE, Cambridge. *Howell Killick Partridge and Amis*. 1970.
Award: Civic Trust Award 1971.
⇌ Cambridge ☏ Bursar 0223 51761

Darwin College has two extensions. One is a very successful terraced infill between two existing buildings, which is uncompromisingly modern yet absolutely right in scale. But the other, the dining room, though superbly detailed in concrete and brick, does not have the same happy relationship with the street or the neighbouring buildings. It is perhaps a building for another place, though the interior, with its characteristic use of mirrors, works well. Conversion work by HKPA in the existing college buildings is a delight to see, though sadly has not been continued throughout the complex.

Cambridge
DOWNING COLLEGE, Cambridge. *Howell Killick Partridge and Amis*. 1970.
Awards: Concrete Society Award 1970; RIBA Award 1971.
⇌ Cambridge ☏ Bursar 0223 59491

This building can only be described as a little gem. The clever design conceals a large block of new buildings containing kitchens and offices, allowing the Combination Room to take all the limelight alongside the original William Wilkins building. The interior of the Combination Room demonstrates the skill of combining a modern building with traditional furniture. It is a building to provide delight in all conditions.

Cambridge
FACULTY OF HISTORY LIBRARY, West Road, Cambridge. *James Stirling and Partner*. 1968.
Award: RIBA Award 1970.
⇌ Cambridge ☏ 0223 61441 (closed weekends)

Representing one of the most exciting periods of Stirling's work, the history library is Cambridge's best known modern building. Two wings contain administrative and teaching accommodation. The glazed library and reading room fan out from between the angled wings. Technical problems have taken a long time to resolve and inevitably detract from its wide acceptability. But the building still has an undeniable sparkle and presence.

Cambridge
GEORGE THOMSON BUILDING, Leckhampton House, Corpus Christi College, Grange Road, Cambridge. *Arup Associates*. 1964.
Award: Civic Trust Award 1965.
⇌ Cambridge ☏ Bursar 0223 59418

This is one of a series of Oxbridge buildings using an exposed external concrete frame to cradle the accommodation. Set in the garden of a late Victorian house, Leckhampton House is a community of postgraduate students. Two residential wings are linked by a stepped mezzanine block containing service areas. The precast structure is detailed to prevent water staining and allows for generous but shaded windows, giving at once a sense of enclosure and release.

16

17

18

19

Cambridge
HARVEY COURT RESIDENTIAL BUILDING, Gonville and Caius College, West Road, Cambridge. *Sir Leslie Martin and Colin St John Wilson.* 1961.
➤ Cambridge

The stepped section of this courtyard scheme allows generous balconies for each of the study bedrooms. On three sides the rooms face inwards overlooking the roof of the submerged breakfast room, while on the fourth side they look onto a mature garden. The colonnade of the West Road evelation is formed by the stepped section and the lower floors giving limited views to the access ways around the perimeter. Brick is used throughout and the building is a successful example of the use of a single material.

Cambridge
HIGHSETT HOUSING, Hills Road, Cambridge. *Eric Lyons Cunningham Partnership.* 1960–1965.
Awards: Phase 2: DoE Housing Award 1964.
    Phase 3: DoE Housing Award 1965; RIBA Award 1966.
➤ Cambridge

One seldom finds a development spanning a long period where successive architectural styles can stand together and gain such high levels of recognition. This scheme was developed in three distinct phases with the basic theme of surrounding a landscaped bowl. Phase 1 comprised three-storey flats in the college quad tradition; Phase 2 added three terraces of two-storey housing; and Phase 3 provided a range of two- and three-storey houses. Finally the central bowl was remodelled with softened banks and planting to create a secret garden separated from the housing groups.

Cambridge
KEELSON, Hills Avenue, Cambridge. *Eric Sorensen.* 1961.
➤ Cambridge

It is rare to find a private house designed by a foreign architect, but here the result is extremely successful. This single storey house relies for its privacy on a series of courtyards overlooked through glazed walling which creates a spacious, light interior. The building has weathered well, the simple overhanging eaves having withstood the rigours of the British climate. Other private houses in the area worth a visit include the Wilson House in Grantchester Road, the Echenique House in Chesterton Road, the Yakeley House in Linton, the Owers House at Stapleford, the Furness House in Hills Avenue and the Thurlow House in Sylvester Road.

Cambridge
KETTLES YARD GALLERY, Northampton Street, Cambridge. *Sir Leslie Martin and David Owers, later with Ivor Richards.* 1970 onwards.
➤ Cambridge ☎ Curator 0223 352124

Built in two stages, the art gallery is an extension to the original house. The simplicity and light tones of the interior allow the exhibits to be viewed in spaces of a sympathetic scale. The experience is more that of visiting a large house than a formal gallery. Externally, reclaimed local bricks are combined with dark stained timber boarding to create a scale which complements neighbouring buildings. Though built with very limited funds, the whole gallery demonstrates how good design can be achieved using the simplest materials.

20

21

22

23

Cambridge
NEW COURT, Christ's College, King Street, Cambridge. *Sir Denys Lasdun, Redhouse and Softley.* 1970.

≋ Cambridge ☎ Bursar 0223 67641

Conceived as the first phase of a residential and sports complex, this building has clear links with the accommodation blocks of the University of East Anglia. The need in Cambridge for a more intimate response to the setting is achieved at the lower levels, but the overall effect is somewhat aloof. External detailing is unconventional, but very successful in allowing roof spaces to be used as sitting out areas. Had the scheme been completed the garden aspect would have benefited, but the decision to call a halt has at least saved King Street from further abuse.

Cambridge
MUSIC SCHOOL, University of Cambridge, off West Road, Cambridge. *Sir Leslie Martin with Colen Lumley and Ivor Richards.* 1978 onwards.

≋ Cambridge ☎ 0223 61661

Starkly simplistic with its buff bricks and zinc roofs, this building was built in phases to include an auditorium and teaching and practice rooms. The interior is simple, and the fine, light touch of the detailing is successful in every aspect of the functional design. It is best to combine a visit to the School with the enjoyment of a public concert.

Cambridge
NEW HALL COLLEGE, Huntington Road, Cambridge. *Chamberlin, Powell and Bon.* 1966.

≋ Cambridge ☎ Bursar 0223 51721

The plan for this college is intended to create a sequence of spaces varying in form and character, with the central sunken court as its focus. The design was geared to unite the various components of the dining hall and library to the residential blocks, and to this end exposed concrete was used for internal and external finishes. With only part of the project completed, the complex is left with a badly defined entrance, but it is hoped that this will be remedied at a later stage.

Cambridge
NEW MUSEUMS BUILDING, Corn Exchange Street, Cambridge. *Arup Associates.* 1971.

Award: RIBA Award 1974.

≋ Cambridge ☎ Director, University Estate Management 0223 59781

One of the last buildings by Arup Associates with an expressed concrete frame, this complex houses the Zoology and Metallurgy Departments and the Computer Laboratory. It features a raised pedestrian deck extending under the three-storey building, giving access to the lecture theatre and views down to the Zoology Museum. The stepped section provides sun screening to the lower floors, while the top storey has internal courtyards.

24

25

26

27

Cambridge
NORTH COURT, JESUS COLLEGE, Cambridge. *David Roberts*. 1965.
≥ Cambridge ☎ Bursar 0223 68611

This building demonstrates Roberts' interest in the relationship between diagonals and interlinking squares, which reappears in the buildings for Trinity down Grange Road. At Jesus, the language of the Modern Movement produces extremely high quality accommodation, the cleverly used materials sustaining their brightness. Roberts reached a number of peaks during his career and this building surely represents one of them.

Cambridge
QUEENSWAY HOUSING, Trumpington Road, Cambridge. *Cambridge Design*. 1978.
Awards: DoE Housing Commendation 1979; RIBA Commendation 1980.
≥ Cambridge

Although firmly in the tradition of deck access housing, this scheme manages to avoid the problems associated with its precedents. This is achieved through a scale limited to three storeys, pleasant landscaped surroundings and architectural restraint. Much of the success is due to the familiar Cambridge Design motifs, particularly the stained timber and concrete balconies set against austere but well proportioned brick walls. Also worth a visit are the practice's other housing schemes in the area: Grasmere Gardens at Carlyle Road, Midwinter Place on Hamilton Road, Lammas Field at Newnham and Shelly Row.

Cambridge
ROBINSON COLLEGE, Grange Road, Cambridge. *Gillespie, Kidd and Coia with YRM*. 1980.
≥ Cambridge ☎ 0223 311431

Though controversial at its inception, this fine building is now settling into a well-formed landscape. The complex comprises residential units, dining and recreation facilities, as well as an elegant library and chapel with a superb window by John Piper. Access is via a gentle ramp from the street which runs through a gateway and so around the college. Inside the walls is a new garden with a small lake through which the Bin Brook flows. Materials used are robust, but the detailing contains a rich range of forms used consistently throughout.

Cambridge
SCHOOL OF ARCHITECTURE EXTENSION, Scroope Terrace, Trumpington Street, Cambridge. *Colin St John Wilson*. 1959.
≥ Cambridge ☎ 0223 69501

Very much of its time, this extension is an essay in brick, concrete and timber and is best seen in the context of Stirling and Gowan's work at Ham Common. Particularly successful is the combination of structural roof elements with a top lighting system to the lecture hall and criticism area. In the former, natural lighting is controlled by an ingenious system of shutters. The central concrete seat shown in early photographs has been removed from the ground floor "pit" along with the original floor matting. As a result the area has lost some of its robustness in an attempt to improve flexibility.

28

29

30

31

Cambridge

SINGLE PERSON HOUSING, 18 and 20 Joan Street, Cambridge. *Keith Garbett*. 1978.

≢ Cambridge ⟺ to Drummer Street

Catering for single women over 40, this small development uses a well-tried vocabulary of form and construction found elsewhere in the city. A firm street façade is balanced by a softer elevation including timber balconies to the south. Brick and timber details and colours are similar to those used for an office development in Round Church Street and on a particularly successful house extension overlooking the cricket ground at Fenners. Garbett's preoccupation with form and light is also illustrated by the Rubbio's house in St Peter's Street.

Cambridge

SPRING HOUSE, Conduit Head Road, Cambridge. *Colin St John Wilson*. 1966.

⟺ off Madingly Road ≢ Cambridge

This private house consists of a simple but rich combination of timber structure and reclaimed Cambridge stock brick walls. A modest porchway opens onto a generous internal space, combining ground and first floor circulation routes. The route culminates in a terrace set under the eaves and offering views to the south and west. An external staircase links down to the garden. In the same area are George Checkley's "White House" and "Thurso" and H.C. Hughes' "Salix House".

Cambridge

STONE BUILDING, Peterhouse College, off Trumpington Street, Cambridge. *Sir Leslie Martin and Colin St John Wilson*. 1964.

≢ Cambridge

It was a brave decision to build an eight-storey block in the centre of Cambridge and one justified by the result. Owing much to the influence of Alvar Aalto it provides a useful but unobtrusive landmark from the Cam. Fine views are provided towards Newnham in the west, the staggered façade also looking south towards Grantchester. The structure is of brick crosswalls with brick-faced façades and strip windows.

Cambridge

UNIVERSITY CENTRE, Granta Place, Cambridge. *Howell Killick Partridge and Amis*. 1967.

Award: Civic Trust Award 1968.

≢ Cambridge ☎ 0223 58933

Housing dining and social facilities for graduates, this building occupies an ideal site overlooking the mill race and pool. The precast concrete frame is finely engineered, gaining stability from the in-situ stairs and lift towers. The stone cladding fixed with stainless steel bolts suggests an armadillo-like character. A number of unusual internal features include the top lit dining hall with its exposed roof trusses and surrounding lounge. The building is well used and has withstood much hard wear.

32

33

34

35

Cambridge

WOLFSON COURT, Girton College, Clarkson Road, Cambridge. *David Roberts and Geoffrey Clarke.* 1971.

⇌ Cambridge ☎ Bursar 0223 311566

Built about three miles away from the main college complex, this block was conceived at a time when isolation and security were considered important. This tends to give it greater legibility as a scheme. Italian influence is evident in the simple red roofs and punctuated brick walls now covered with rich planting. Within the walls a series of courtyard spaces have an almost cloistered feeling, providing a fine, sheltered environment for the residents.

Colchester

TREBOR FACTORY, Severalls Lane Industrial Estate, Colchester, Essex. *Arup Associates.* 1980.

Awards: Business and Industry Award 1982. RIBA Award 1983.

🚗 A12 to Colchester; two miles NE of town centre ⇌ Colchester ☎ 0206 844333

The brief called for an overall identity linking different production areas with provision for future expansion. Separate elements house the different activities with the main circulation street forming the lifeline of service distribution. The production pavilions follow a structural grid, each one characterised by a concrete pyramid with a rooflight at its centre. Windows are as large as energy conservation requirements would allow. Sugar silos and the boiler house occupy a key position at the centre of the complex.

Colchester

WEDGWOOD HOUSE, Ketelfield, Higham St Mary, Colchester. *Aldington, Craig and Collinge.* 1977.

Award: RIBA Commendation 1978.

🚗 off Colchester By Pass between Colchester and Ipswich ⇌ Colchester ☎ 0844 291228

This steel and glass pavilion inevitably invites comparison with Mies van der Rohe's Farnsworth House. The simple rectangular form is raised above the ground with a separate terrace on an intermediate level and steps to the garden. The house settles a little uncomfortably between the Miesian image and the more traditional designs of this practice's earlier houses, never quite achieving the simplicity to make it entirely successful. But its response to the landscape is undeniably acceptable.

Cottered

THE GARDEN HOUSE, Cottered, Hertfordshire. *The Charter Partnership.* 1968.

🚗 along Buntingford Road ☎ 0234 42551

This house is set in a classical Japanese garden devised by a rich merchant earlier this century. To honour its surroundings, the house is conceived as a single storey, timber framed building with red cedar boarding and cedar roof shingles. The living space on the upper level has superb views across the gardens. Beneath are service and storage facilities.

36

37

38

39

Great Waldingfield

GREAT WALDINGFIELD PRIMARY SCHOOL, Great Waldingfield, Suffolk. *Suffolk County Architects.* 1970.

Award: Civic Trust Commendation 1971.

🚌 B1115 from Sudbury 🚌 from Sudbury to Waldingfield.

One of Jack Digby's first projects as County Architect, this school displays a freshness of approach and sets standards that were followed in successful buildings throughout West Suffolk.

A space-frame roof supported on steel columns and independent of the brick walls contrasts well with the rural landscape enhanced by the scheme's own planting. Another local school by Digby is Hartest Primary School and this too is worth a visit.

Hunstanton

HUNSTANTON SCHOOL, Downs Road, Hunstanton. *Alison and Peter Smithson.* 1954.

🚌 off the Kings Lynn to Hunstanton road ≽ Kings Lynn ☏ Headmaster 04853 2481

Substantial alterations are changing the character of this most famous Brutalist building. The competition winning design has suffered heavy rusting due to its proximity to the sea. It is expensive on energy and the underfloor heating in conjunction with the glass walls cannot respond to fast-changing external temperatures. The cost of repairs was such that the Norfolk County Council considered demolition. However, the building's architectural reputation saved it.

Ipswich

FISONS 'HARVEST HOUSE' OFFICES, Princess Street, Ipswich. *Johns, Slater and Haward.* 1960.

Award: RIBA Bronze Medal 1961.

≽ Ipswich ☏ 0473 56721

This building demonstrates a simplicity of layout and efficient site use. The buildings are arranged around the perimeter enclosing a pleasant court and pool. This overall strategy incorporating an elegant H-shaped structural system gives a lightness of touch seldom matched.

Ipswich

WILLIS FABER AND DUMAS HEADQUARTERS, Friars Street, Ipswich. *Foster Associates.* 1975.

Awards: Royal Society of Arts Business and Industry Award 1976; R S Reynolds Memorial Award 1976; RIBA Award 1977.

≽ Ipswich ☏ 0473 217911

This is a stunning building which protects the privacy of the workforce while allowing public access via the escalators at the core. These link the large roof garden and restaurant pavilion to other public areas and the ground floor. There are many technical innovations, particularly the glass curtain walling which by day reflects the surrounding townscape becoming transparent at night to reveal the finely detailed interiors.

40

41

42

43

Kings Lynn
BESPAK FACTORY AND OFFICES, Berwen Way, Kings Lynn, Norfolk.
Cambridge Design. 1980.
Awards: Structural Steel Commendation 1981; Civic Trust Commendation
1982.
🚌 A148 from Kings Lynn ⇌ Kings Lynn ☎ 0553 62711

This building is a lucid and uncompromised exposition of construction.
Yellow-painted columns provide bracing contrast with the brown cladding
behind, while windows set behind the columns achieve a sense of depth.
Though generally discreet and sensitive, the design has its weaknesses,
such as the indecisive relationship between factory and offices, and the
hipped roof which presents rather than resolves the conflict of technology
and tradition. But what sticks in the memory is the successful reconcilia-
tion of a bold concept with the complexity of the brief.

Melbourn
PATS CENTRE RESEARCH LABORATORY AND OFFICES, Melbourn,
Royston. *Piano and Rogers*. 1975.
🚌 A10 to Melbourn 🚌 from Cambridge to Melbourn ⇌ Cambridge
☎ Administration Manager 0763 61222

Carved into the chalk ground rising to the south of Melbourn, the intention behind this building remains uncertain. It is unclear, particularly from
the entrance, whether the first floor was conceived to float above the hill
with car park and servicing below or whether some other important relationship was meant. This first floor houses research laboratories serviced
from below with ductwork straggling into the undercroft from where the
glazed entrance rises. Though the steel frame, glass and lightweight parti-
tion interiors are well defined, the building lacks the panache for which the
designers are famed.

Meldreth
MELDRETH MANOR SCHOOL, Nr Royston, Cambridge. *Architects Co-
Partnership*. 1965.
🚌 off A10 ☎ Bursar 0763 60771

This building combines the simple ingredients of white-painted brick and
slate roofs which suits the Cambridgeshire countryside. A boarding school
for handicapped children, the complex has been sensitively conceived as
a self-contained village. Apart from the central administrative block, there
are four school houses within an orchard setting, each with its own kitchen
and dining facilities, classrooms, recreation rooms and dormitories. Staff
are housed in a hostel, flats and houses around the perimeter of the site
to allow them privacy when off duty.

Norwich
ARCHITECTS' OFFICES, Ferry Road, Norwich. *Feilden and Mawson*.
1968.
Award: Civic Trust Award 1969.
⇌ Thorpe Station ☎ 0603 29571

Though slotted between two pleasant Edwardian houses, Feilden and
Mawson's offices do not attempt to ape their neighbours, making instead
their own contribution in a well-mannered and dignified way. Other local
buildings by the practice worth a visit include housing at Friars Quay and
buildings on the University of East Anglia campus.

44

45

46

47

Norwich
QUEEN ELIZABETH CLOSE SHELTERED HOUSING, St Martin at Palace Plain, Norwich. *Feilden and Mawson*. 1974.
Awards: DoE Award for Good Design in Housing 1974; RIBA Award 1974; Civic Trust Award 1975.
≥ Norwich

The development of this city centre site for an experienced client has produced an extremely successful building. The existing boundary wall is incorporated into the design using traditional materials and detailing to enhance the building and its surroundings. The scheme demonstrates a control of architectural form and provides an extremely pleasant place to live.

Norwich
THE SAINSBURY CENTRE FOR VISUAL ARTS, University of East Anglia, Norwich. *Foster Associates*. 1978.
Awards: RIBA Award 1978; Structural Steel Finniston Award 1978; R S Reynolds Award 1979; British Tourist Board Award 1979; Sixth International Prize for Architecture, Brussels 1980; Ambrose Congreve Award 1980; Museum of the Year Award 1980.
🚗 M11/A11 via Newmarket and Thetford 🚌 510/556 to University Plain from Castle Meadow ≥ Norwich ☎ 0603 56161 (closed Mondays)

There is a marked contrast between the Sainsbury Centre and the rest of the campus yet the two parts remain in balance. The Centre contains its various functions in a disarmingly appropriate manner. Sophisticated components include aluminium, steel, glass and Neoprene. The clear span structure creates an internal space of cathedral-like grace.

Norwich
UNIVERSITY OF EAST ANGLIA, University Plain, Norwich. *Sir Denys Lasdun and Partners*. 1970.
Award: Civic Trust Award 1969.
🚗 M11/A11 via Newmarket and Thetford 🚌 510/556 to University Plain from Castle Meadow ≥ Norwich ☎ Estates Officer 0603 56161 (closed Mondays)

These, the first permanent buildings on the campus, have set the scene for a number of distinguished practices to make their own contribution to the university complex. Lasdun set out to create "architectural hills and valleys in an evocation of the permanent human environment and identification with nature and the primal dwelling". The classic view from the A11 confirms this intention with stepped ziggurats making the transition from the open rolling landscape to the formal teaching blocks beyond.

Peterborough
KEY THEATRE, Embankment Road, Peterborough. *Mathew Robotham and Quinn*. 1973.
Award: RIBA Commendation 1974.
≥ Peterborough ☎ Director 0733 52437

Set on the banks of the River Nene beside an open tract of land, this pavilion can be viewed from all sides. The combination of pleasant brick, cantilevered upper storey and carefully modelled roof is highly successful. The auditorium containing 400 seats has great intimacy, while the foyer upstairs with its columns and coffered ceilings is an enjoyable place to wait between performances.

48

49

50

51

Snape

THE MALTINGS CONCERT HALL, Snape, Suffolk. *Arup Associates.* 1967.
Award: Civic Trust Award 1968.
🚗 A12 then A1094 to Snape/Aldeburgh 🚉 Festival Office, Aldeburgh 072
885 852935

Commissioned by composer Benjamin Britten, the architects have converted this old malt house into a space the proportions of which equal the best European concert halls. The conversion work was far greater than it appears. The authentic-looking roof is new, as are the modern trusses with members of high tensile steel. New smoke hoods hide the dampers of the mechanical ventilation system. But to sustain the original industrial character materials are used sparingly. Brick walls, grit blasted to reveal their original colour, double as sound absorbers, roof timbers are unpainted and the steel sherardised.

Westoning

MACINTYRE SCHOOL FOR THE MENTALLY HANDICAPPED, Westoning, Beds. *MacCormac, Jamieson and Pritchard.* 1975.
Awards: AD Design Award 1974; RIBA Regional Commendation 1976.
🚉 Flitwick

A series of pavilions in the grounds of Westoning Manor, this school demonstrates the potential of system building. In this case, the Norwegian-born system uses traditional log cabin construction techniques. The pin wheel pavilions with their hipped roofs provide a warm and responsive environment for the handicapped children who live here.

Whittlesey

SUDBURY COURT SHELTERED HOUSING, Stonald Road, Whittlesey, Nr Peterborough. *Mathew Robotham and Quinn.* 1977.
Awards: DoE Award 1979; RIBA Commendation 1979; Civic Trust Award 1980.
🚗 A15/A605 🚉 Warden 0733 204092

This scheme demonstrates how the sensitive use of traditional form and construction can produce a delightful living environment. The warm red bricks and clay pantiles are sympathetic to the scale of the buildings which look on to a beautifully landscaped area. This area also includes allotments, a greenhouse and tenants' gardens. Other housing schemes by this practice in the Peterborough area are worth a visit, notably Oakley Drive, and Ashfields in Peterborough and Lynn Road at Wisbech.

Witham

HURST GUNSON COOPER TABER SEED WAREHOUSE AND PROCESSING BUILDING, Station Road, Witham, Essex. *Chamberlin, Powell and Bon.* 1956.
Award: RIBA Bronze Medal 1957.
🚉 Witham 🚉 0736 516600

The different forms of these two buildings were determined by their functions, the processing plant being active, the warehouse passive. Their relationship is stressed by the proportions and detailing. The processing block is a cubic steel cage set on a blue brick plinth, while the warehouse consists of three clear span concrete platforms identical in plan.

52

53

54

55

East Midlands

Chesterfield
THE PAVEMENTS SHOPPING CENTRE, Market Square, Chesterfield.
Elsom Pack and Roberts Partnership. (Consultants Feilden and Mawson).
1980.
Awards: Europa Nostra Medal 1981; Civic Trust Award 1982.
⇌ Chesterfield
   This central area redevelopment is a good example of sensitive renewal
and rehabilitation. The scheme introduces a new building but respects the
existing grain of the town. The open market place has been retained as a
focus, the rugged Victorian market hall improved and extended and a new
shopping arcade and multi-storey car park added behind the existing
facades on the south side of the square. This, plus the restoration of the
timber framed Peacock Inn, highlights the project as an outstanding civic
improvement.

Derby
OLIVETTI BRANCH OFFICE, Meadows Industrial Estate, Nottingham
Road, Derby. *Edward Cullinan.* 1971.
⊕ A52 ⇌ Derby ☎ 0332 49616
   This scheme is based on a generic form devised by Cullinan for a series
of similar buildings. The largest of the four built, it provides workshop, office and service space arranged on three sides of an enclosed courtyard.
The structure is concrete at ground level with a steel framed upper storey
clad with timber panels. A large roof, tilted to admit light and with triangular
openings in the eaves, is faced with yellow grp. This transforms the building into an assertive and surprising project in a rather dismal setting.

Holbeach
COSIRA FACTORY UNITS, Station Road, Holbeach, Lincs. *Mathew
Robotham and Quinn.* 1979.
⊕ A151 ⊕ from Spalding or Kings Lynn
   This scheme is a good example of architectural ingenuity. Two tiny units
on the outskirts of an agricultural town were carefully designed to re-use
much of the materials of an old seed mill previously on the site. The
monopitch roofs use the old timber king-post trusses and bricks and pine
boarding were reclaimed. Bold detailing of timber doors and porthole windows to the offices show how modest new buildings can fit among old
without the squalor often associated with industrial complexes.

56

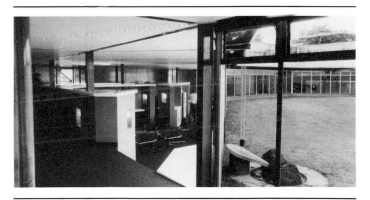

57

58

Leicester
ATTENBOROUGH BUILDING, University of Leicester. *Arup Associates.*
1972.
⇌ Leicester ☎ 0533 554455
 Set on the edge of the campus overlooking Victoria Park, this is one
piece in a distinguished collection of buildings commissioned by the University in the 60s. The complex has three main elements: a tower containing tutorial rooms; a low building including seminar rooms and an ar-
chaeological laboratory; and three lecture halls beneath the external terraces. The light brown brick at ground level and for terracing is the same
as is used widely throughout the campus. White precast concrete cladding
is used on the tower, punctuated by projecting windows designed for natural ventilation.

Leicester
ENGINEERING BUILDING, Leicester University. *James Stirling and James
Gowan.* 1963.
Award: R S Reynolds Award 1964.
⇌ Leicester ☎ Registrar 0533 50000
 One of the most influential post-war buildings, this complex is designed
to express its component parts. Glazed offices tower above the brick-tiled
lecture theatre with laboratories in a separate tower. Workshops run along
the side in a low brick-faced shed with serrated north light translucent roof.
Services are firmly pulled away making another series of towers. The
whole composition seems to derive directly from the Victorian industrial
form. Generally the building has weathered well and has been properly
maintained.

Leicester
UNIVERSITY LIBRARY, Leicester. *Castle Park Dean Hook.* 1974.
⇌ Leicester ☎ 0533 554455
 A restrained glass clad block, the library is overlooked by the Worth-
ington Building and Stirling and Gowan's engineering block so its
roofscape is important. The area acts as a visual reflector and thermal
stabiliser with glazed aisles affording access to rooftop services. Externally, the building fits its setting. Services are integrated into the fabric with
precast double tee beams and hollow in-situ columns acting as ducts. Inside, the concrete structure eliminates the need for suspended ceilings,
but the interiors are poorly fitted out. Old furniture and makeshift graphics
create a series of bleak and disappointing spaces.

Loughborough
LOUGHBOROUGH UNIVERSITY, Ashby Road, Loughborough, Leics.
Arup Associates, 1970.
⇌ Loughborough ⇌ A512 on west side of town
 In 1966 Arup Associates prepared a master plan for the development of
an existing college with 1,500 students into a university of 5,000 students.
The plan attempted to establish a discipline which would allow for growth
and change, and proposed a system of planning and construction based on
a series of dimensional grids. The building is based on a standard 15.2 m
grid alternating with a 4.5 m communications strip. The building expresses
its parts and is finely detailed; but the University has only partially adopted
the master plan, and the contrasts are obvious.

59

60

61

62

Newark
BARNBY ROAD INFANTS SCHOOL, Cromwell Road, Newark. *Nottinghamshire County Architects*. 1959.

➤ Newark ☎ Head Teacher 0636 2115

This three-classroom school was one of the first in Nottinghamshire to use the Mark 2 CLASP system and after almost 25 years it remains virtually unchanged. Developed originally to withstand mining subsidence, the system can also be used, as it is here, on non-subsidence sites. It uses factory-made components and a dry construction system and is geared to rapid site assembly. Though it has been improved over the years, the system still forms the basis for a number of public building types, including schools, clinics and health centres.

Northampton
CARLSBERG BREWERY, St Peter's Way, Northampton. *Knud Munk*. 1973-79.

➤ Northampton ☎ 0604 21621

Constructed in four stages, a single building houses the brewhouse and energy centre, fermenting area, canning and packaging hall. Unlike many industrial buildings, the brewery expresses its parts clearly, culminating in a spectacular glazed hall on the banks of the River Nene. Two concrete flank walls step up over the energy centre and brewhouse to give it its distinctive silhouette. Treatment tanks are planned clear of the main block in serried ranks along the western side. The brewhouse is the centrepiece, the plant being visible day and night behind a giant faceted window on the south façade.

Nottingham
BOOTS HEAD OFFICE, Beeston, Nottingham. *Skidmore Owings and Merrill with Yorke Rosenberg and Mardall*. 1968.

🚌 A614 ➤ Nottingham ☎ 0602 56111

This elegant block sits at the entrance to the Boots complex close by Sir Owen Williams' 30s reinforced concrete manufacturing buildings. It is a formal single-storey glass pavilion with external structural frame. A central paved courtyard admits natural light to the offices and lower floor. The thorough ordering of the building and meticulous detailing hints at SOM's influence, extending inside to the internal planning and choice of furnishings.

Nottingham
HORIZON FACTORY, JOHN PLAYER AND SONS, Beeston, Nottingham. *Arup Associates*. 1971.

Award: RIBA Award 1972.

🚌 A614. ➤ Nottingham 🚌 46, 47, 48 ☎ Nottingham 0602 787711

This cigarette factory is a prototype for the modern flexible industrial building. It provides large column-free spaces with very heavy floor loadings, generous service areas and high security. The design is based on a four-layered 30 m structural grid and features walk-in service floors above and below the main production area at second floor level. Structural elements are articulated in an elegant and considered manner. A total energy plant is incorporated using gas turbine alternator sets. The project pioneered the use of management contract, for the speedy construction of complex buildings.

63

64

65

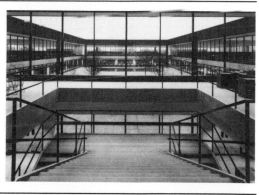

66

Nottingham
NOTTINGHAM PLAYHOUSE, Wellington Circus, Nottingham. *Peter Moro Partnership*. 1963.
Awards: RIBA Award 1964; Civic Trust Award 1965.
⇌ Nottingham ☎ 0602 44361

This is one of the first and best of the 60s regional theatres. Seating 750, the auditorium is contained within a distinct drum with the proscenium formed by cutting out a section of the drumwall. Open foyer spaces arranged around the perimeter open out onto Wellington Square. A bar and restaurant are housed in a single storey block linked to the foyers. The resident company is noted for its productions, and visitors to the building should also buy a ticket for the play!

Nottingham
THEATRE ROYAL AND ROYAL CONCERT HALL, Upper Parliament Street, Nottingham. *Renton Howard Wood Levin Partnership*. 1978 and 1983.
Award: RIBA Award 1979 (Theatre Royal).
⇌ Nottingham ☎ 0602 42328

Substantial new buildings were added to C.J. Phipps' theatre, extensively altered by Frank Matcham. The fine portico and auditorium were retained but white mosaic clad curved walls enclose new front of house and backstage facilities. The concert hall is linked to the theatre by the same curving walls and is designed for flexibility. Entrance foyers are set behind a rippling glass façade finished as a blue-framed screen with dramatic neon sculptures tumbling over the building to mark the entrance. Inside the concert hall is a movable acoustic canopy, the largest in the world.

Tibshelf
SAPA FACTORY AND OFFICES, Sawpit Lane, Tibshelf, Derbyshire. *Foster Associates (factory) and Wm Saunders and Partners (offices)*. 1977 and 1979.
Award: Office of the Year Award 1980.
🚗 M1/B6014 🚌 from Mansfield and Chesterfield 331 or 341 ☎ 0773 872761

Set on a dreary industrial estate, the factory houses a printing press and support facilities. Inside the bland white box, the structure, services and plant are coloured to respond to the visible spectrum of the artificial lighting. The offices in a steel framed glass box are separate but linked to the factory. Although it appears single storey, the office block has basement accommodation giving 800 sq m in all. The complex is an impressive attempt by the client to upgrade the design of industrial buildings.

Wirksworth
JUBILEE COURT HOUSING, Kingsfield Road, Wirksworth, Derbyshire. *Sebire and Allsopp*. 1976.
Awards: Civic Trust Commendation 1978; Eternit Award 1978; DoE Good Design in Housing Award 1978.
🚗 off A6 on Ashbourne Road 🚌 from Alfreton 240, 241

Comprising 20 new houses on the edge of the town, this development has three blocks of two-storey brick terraces in a picturesque rural setting. Together with an existing terrace, these are arranged to form an inner entrance courtyard but retain fine views across the Derbyshire countryside from living rooms. A four-metre fall across the site has been exploited to produce a fragmented building form with a series of monopitch slate roofs. Wirksworth itself has been regenerated largely through self-help and initiative projects, winning a Europa Nostra Medal in 1982.

67

68

69

70

London

City
BARBICAN COMPLEX (HOUSING, SCHOOLS, ARTS AND CONFER-
ENCES), Barbican, EC2. *Chamberlin, Powell and Bon.* Completed 1982.
Award: RIBA Award 1974 (St Giles churchyard)
⊖ Barbican or Moorgate ☎ Housing 01-628 4341; Arts and Conference
Centre 01-638 4141
 Conceived over 25 years ago, this is a rare example of contemporary
architecture which uses a Grand Plan. Exposed reinforced concrete is used
throughout, from the 40-storey residential tower blocks to the Arts Centre
on Silk Street. Detailing is heavy-handed, with largely prefabricated components and little relief to humanise the complex. When wet the concrete
streaks, but when the sun is out the sculptural design of the towers comes
into its own. The Arts Centre is notoriously difficult to find, but the Conservatory, Frobisher Crescent make the trip worthwhile.

City
BUSH LANE HOUSE OFFICES, 80 Cannon Street, EC4. *Arup Associates.*
1976.
Award: Structural Steel Award 1977
⇌ Cannon Street ⊖ Cannon Street
 When this building was designed a section of the Underground was to
run underneath. To reduce foundations the architects evolved a cantilevered structure with minimum supports. Above the first floor plant
rooms a tubular lattice "exoskeleton" supports the offices, giving column-
free interiors. The stainless steel skeleton is water-filled to comply with fire
regulations. Behind is a tinted double glazed curtain wall.
 This is a striking building, far superior to most speculative City offices.
It matters not that the Jubilee Line extension has been abandoned, depriv-
ing it of its principal raison d'etre.

City
COMMERCIAL UNION AND PENINSULA AND ORIENTAL STEAM NAVI-
GATION COMPANY OFFICES, Leadenhall Street, EC3. *GMW Partnership.*
1969 and 1968.
Awards: Structural Steel Award 1970; Civic Trust Award 1970
⊖ Bank
 The P and O with its tower and podium is typical of mid-60s office developments. The podium offered an acceptable streetscape and deep-plan
shopping units at ground level. But though this was one of the most elegant examples of that style, now the projecting floor slabs and square proportions make it seem inelegant and fussy. The detailing of the Commercial
Union is immaculate and sets it apart from its contemporaries, establishing
a standard which few comparable buildings have since matched.

71

72

73

City

CREDIT LYONNAIS BANK, 84/94 Queen Victoria Street, EC4. *The Whinney Mackay-Lewis Partnership.* 1980.
Award: Evening Standard Popularity Poll 1979.
⊖ Mansion House ☎ 01-248 9696

Credit Lyonnais is an architectural enigma with several unusual features. It leans outwards at each storey, thereby increasing the total floor area; and it is one of the first buildings to use glass-reinforced cement cladding panels into which are set coffin-shaped windows. On the top floor the panels appear to have been installed upside down giving the building a curiously unfinished appearance. It was built in record time and has weathered well. The interiors are garish and fussy with lavish use of expensive materials.

City

GUILDHALL EXTENSION AND PRECINCTS, Guildhall, EC2. *Sir Giles Scott Son and Partner.* 1974.
⊖ Bank or Moorgate ☎ 01-606 3030 (library and art gallery)

The practice's work on the Guildhall spans 30 years. The municipal offices built between 1955–58 are, according to Pevsner, "of light brick and painfully antiquated, with 20s motifs along the ground floor and corrugated top frieze." The L-shaped extension clad in pre-cast concrete is now similarly dated with its motif of pointed heads and concrete umbrellas. The precincts connect to upper pedestrian levels of the Barbican and are notable for the disjunction between street pattern and Barbican grid.

City

LLOYD'S OF LONDON INSURANCE MARKET AND OFFICES, Lime Street, EC3. *Richard Rogers and Partners.* Completion late 1985.
⊖ Bank

When completed, this 50,000 sq m block will be the City's most outstanding new building. Rogers has turned conventional building inside out, placing lifts stairs and services in six satellite towers around the perimeter.

The focal point is The Room, a vast market area above which will be a central atrium. External cladding will consist of triple glazing through which surplus warm air will pass to aid thermal efficiency. In contrast to the high technology, the pedimented entrance to the 1925 Lloyd's building is to be retained.

City

NATIONAL WESTMINSTER BANK TOWER, 25 Old Broad St, EC2. *Richard Seifert and Partners.* 1981.
Awards: European Steel Award 1981; RIBA Commendation 1983.
⊖ Bank

Britain's tallest tower block at 183 m high, the building's plan shape is quixotically based on the Bank's motif. The RIBA's citation reads: "The architects have created a design of individual character on the London skyline with slim proportions and an envelope of lasting quality. New techniques of slipform cores and cantilevered floors have enabled the design team to create a fluid expression in the façades."

74

75

76

77

City

ST KATHARINE'S DOCK HOUSE, St Katharine's Dock, EC1, *Andrew Renton and Associates*. 1965.

⇌ Fenchurch Street ⊖ Tower Hill

For the main opus, Renton wanted a building "not compromised and browbeaten by the old", but complementing the existing warehouses by Philip Hardwicke and Telford's St Katharine's Dock. In the event, Hardwicke's fire-damaged Warehouse B has been rebuilt in red rather than brown brick, and together with an indifferent speculative office block constitutes the World Trade Centre. Other buildings include GLC housing in St Katharine's Way and the 200-year-old timber frame Dickens Inn. The Dock is worth a visit if only as an example of the mediocre approach to revitalising London's Docklands.

West End

BRUNSWICK CENTRE, Bernard Street, WC1. *Patrick Hodgkinson*. 1973.

⊖ Russell Square

One of the earlier examples of 70s urban megastructures, the Brunswick Centre is uncompromising *béton brut*, largely unsoftened by the passage of time. The stepped arrangement of housing above shops to either side of a pedestrian plaza became a much imitated form. Despite its bulk it fits discreetly into its corner of Bloomsbury, not shouting its presence above the rooftops. To see it at its worst, go on a wet, windy day. But on the good side are details such as the little conservatories on the housing balconies and its overall success in achieving a self-sufficient community.

West End

CENTRE POINT OFFICES, New Oxford Street, WC1. *Richard Seifert and Partners*. 1971.

⊖ Tottenham Court Road ☎ 01-379 7400

A true London landmark, Seifert's elegant tower gained notoriety when built for remaining doggedly unlet. (It was finally occupied by the Confederation of British Industry.) Erected rapidly with precast cladding components, it displays the Seifert motif of honeycombed window detailing. Space planners may criticise it for being too slim for its concrete core and its cantilevered floor construction, which leaves relatively little square footage per floor. The plaza with fountains is no place to linger because of the traffic which isolates it, but its dinosaur legs raise a smile. Stunning when floodlit in the early evening.

West End

CLIFTON NURSERIES GARDEN CENTRES, The Colonnades, Bishops Bridge Road, W2 and 16 Russell Street, WC2. *Terry Farrell Partnership*. 1980; 1981.

Colonnades: ⇌ Paddington ⊖ Paddington ☎ 01-402 9834. Covent Garden: ⇌ Charing Cross ⊖ Covent Garden (closed Sunday) Holborn, Charing Cross or Leicester Square ☎ 01-379 6878

As the first truly flamboyant building from Terry Farrell after his split with Nick Grimshaw, the Colonnades conservatory retains some notoriety, sitting adjacent to shops and offices designed by the pair. But its Covent Garden sister (*see picture*) is more adept at mixing stylistic metaphors and tongue-in-cheek historicism typical of British Post-modernism. Both buildings highlight Farrell's ability to combine technological innovation with fancy.

78

79

80

81

West End
COLLEGE OF ENGINEERING AND SCIENCE, POLYTECHNIC OF CEN-
TRAL LONDON, New Cavendish Street, W1. *Lyons Israel Ellis*. 1970.
⊖ Goodge Street or Oxford Circus ☎ 01-486 5811

Occupying a city block, the complex is outward looking on four sides. A
small lecture hall is fashionably cantilevered over the main entrance. Exposed shutter-board concrete is used for the cantilevers and lift shafts with
elegant bronze curtain walling cladding communal and terraced areas.
Cream brick paviors face the raised podium over the basement car park.
Detailing has been carried out with assurance and conviction, but the complex has been poorly maintained and badly needs a clean.

West End
COUTTS BANK, 440 The Strand, WC2. *Frederick Gibberd and Partners*.
1980.
≋ Charing Cross ⊖ Charing Cross ☎ 01-379 6262

Previously decrepit, this Nash building has become the shell for a modern banking office. Nash's genius is present in the "pepperpots", carefully
contrived to turn the corners of this angular building from any viewpoint.
The new building within the Nash façade shows through in a dramatic entrance atrium. The development has a slightly unreal quality, being apparently undermined by vast subways; nonetheless, it is one of the best examples of an historic building imaginatively adapted to a new use.

West End
COVENT GARDEN MARKET HALL, Covent Garden Piazza, WC2. *GLC De-
partment of Architecture and Civic Design: Historic Buildings Division*.
1980.
≋ Charing Cross ⊖ Covent Garden (closed Sundays), Holborn, Charing
Cross or Leicester Square

Charles Fowler's original building, completed in 1830, was abandoned in
1974 when the fruit and vegetable market moved to Nine Elms. It is now
converted to shops, restaurants and offices and thrives beyond the GLC's
wildest hopes. This is a very conscientious restoration, immaculately exe-
cuted. The only adaptation to the original is the excavation of new courtyards to open part of the basement area for public use and to increase retail
space.

West End
COVENT GARDEN REDEVELOPMENT, WC2. *Various architects*. 1968 onwards.
≋ Charing Cross ⊖ Leicester Square, Embankment or Covent Garden
(closed Sundays)

Refurbishment has virtually replaced new build since the original redevelopment plans of 1968 were scuppered by community pressure. Only
Thorn House (Sir Basil Spence 1960) remains, ignoring the street lines except in its two-storey podium. Richard Seifert and Partners offer speculative examples nearby in Centre Point (p. 42), their own bland brick offices
in Shaftesbury Avenue and more sophisticated marble-clad offices in Long
Acre. Adjacent to the latter is the GLC's Odhams Walk housing scheme
(1982). Also worth a glance are GMW's Opera House Extension in James
Street and Powell and Moya's mixed development in Endell Street.

82

83

84

85

West End

INSTITUTES OF EDUCATION AND LAW, Bedford Way, WC1. *Sir Denys Lasdun and Partners*. 1976.

⊖ Russell Square ☏ 01-636 1500

This is a building of great pure forms, its flank down Bedford Way recalling passenger liners or spacecraft. Glossy curtain walling provides an essentially rectilinear, horizontally banded structure, separated by massive abstract concrete forms. The building must be appreciated in its own right as a piece of sculpture, for it certainly makes no concessions to the domestic scale of neighbouring buildings. It has its weak points, especially towards the rear, but remains an uncompromisingly beautiful building.

West End

LONDON TELECOM TOWER, Cleveland Street, W1. *Ministry of Public Building and Works (now DoE/PSA)*. 1966.

⊖ Warren Street or Great Portland Street ☏ 01-636 7202

Despite its ham-fisted detailing, this is a charming landmark on London's skyline. Though similar to other telecommunications towers throughout the country, it has the added features of a revolving restaurant around the top (now closed after a terrorist attack), and plant rooms around the main structure, both clad in seemingly off-the-peg curtain walling. This utilitarian approach may explain why it has not come to represent London's image in the way similar, more exotic towers do for other major cities. At 174 m it was London's tallest structure until the completion of the NatWest Tower (p. 40).

West End

PICCADILLY CIRCUS REDEVELOPMENT, W1. *Various architects*.

⊖ Piccadilly Circus

One of the longest urban planning sagas, Piccadilly Circus has suffered from planning blight. Attempts to divert traffic or deck it over for pedestrians have long been aborted and its chaotic character will remain. Piecemeal redevelopment is proceeding with Powell, Moya and Partners' NatWest Bank at 19-23 Shaftesbury Avenue (1982), Sir John Burnet Tait and Partners' building at 44-48 Regent Street and Fitzroy Robinson Partnership's massive infill on the Trocadero site (1983). The new Trocadero is an entertainment complex with shopping, restaurants and leisure facilities on several levels, grouped around a central atrium. The new building emerges from the centre of the site with new façades onto each of the four surrounding streets.

West End

TUC BUILDING, Great Russell Street, WC1. *David Du R. Aberdeen*. 1957.

⊖ Tottenham Court Road ☏ 01-636 4030

The eye is first caught by the entrance sculpture and then by the Lubetkin-like window arrangement on the main façade. Lubetkin's influence continues strongly along Dyott Street with a stack of purely ornamental steel and glass balconies. This east elevation is the most interesting as the mass is broken down in several ways – by a semicircular glazed stairwell, a jettied first floor and Odeon-style curved walls above. Attention to detail is gratifying. Now something of a period piece, the building has weathered comparatively well and still exudes a confident air.

86

87

88

89

West End

UNITED STATES EMBASSY, Grosvenor Square, W1. *Eero Saarinen*. 1960.
⊖ Bond Street.

Saarinen's building, which dominates Grosvenor Square, was the subject of considerable controversy during its construction. Its monumental design, while reflecting its diplomatic purpose, is somehow alien to the terraced continuity of the grand buildings making up the rest of the square. The brash articulation of its main façade and lavish use of gilt somehow symbolises America and the gold eagle on the roof line is a suitable totem. Not one of Saarinen's best buildings, the Embassy has not mellowed with age. It it has become accepted as a familiar monument though remaining something of an intruder.

East

ASH GROVE BUS GARAGE, Ash Grove, E8. *London Transport Executive Architect's Department*. 1981.
≋ Cambridge Heath ⊖ Bethnal Green ☎ 01-254 1354

The first of London Transport's latest batch of bus garages, Ash Grove is surprisingly unobtrusive for its size. A single storey brick wall encloses garage, workshops, car parking, operating block and external bus park. Best feature is the roof, only visible in its entirety within the garage space, where trusses span up to 54 m.

East

OLSEN BUILDING, Millwall Dock, E14. *Foster Associates*. 1969.
Awards: Architectural Design Projects Award 1969; Financial Times Architectural Award 1970.
⬛ A13 then A1206 at Limehouse to Isle of Dogs ⬛ 56 (Mon-Sat) or 277 ⊖ Mile End ☎ London Docklands Development Corporation 01-515 3000

Originally designed as an amenity building and operations centre for the Fred Olsen shipping line, this unit neatly slots into a 27.5 m gap between two widespan sheds designed by the Port of London Authority. It was completed within a nine-month design-and-build contract. Current occupants are the London Docklands Development Corporation who see the building as a showpiece for future office and warehouse developments in the Docklands area.

East

ROBIN HOOD GARDENS HOUSING, Robin Hood Lane, Poplar, E14. *Alison and Peter Smithson*. 1972.
⊖ Bromley by Bow

Consisting of two curving slab blocks, eight and ten storeys high, this scheme provides around 200 deck access maisonettes. Though from a distance it appears as a powerful and subtle piece of sculpture, it has suffered from vandalism and from the tawdriness of its many indefensible spaces. The surfaces have worn better than most, but its overall impact is that of a very drab, oversize chunk of concrete.

90

91

92

93

East

ST PAUL'S PRIMARY SCHOOL, Leopold Street, E3. *Maguire and Murray.* 1972.

≩ Stepney East ⊖ Mile End ☎ 01-987 4624

Probably one of the best examples of post-war primary school planning, the design centres on the "home-base" teaching system which combines open plan and classroom accommodation. By using a portal frame agricultural shed, the architects achieved almost 20 per cent more space per child than is standard within cost limits. Unfortunately the building hasn't weathered well and is nicknamed "the pig sty". Also on the site is St Paul's Church which launched Maguire and Murray's reputation in the late 50s and helped set the pattern for modern ecclesiastical design.

East

TRUMAN BREWERY, 9 Brick Lane, E1. *Arup Associates.* 1976.

Awards: Business and Industrial Award 1976; Financial Times Commendation 1977; RIBA Commendation 1981.

≩ Fenchurch Street ⊖ Aldgate East ☎ Company Secretary 01-247 4300

Three storeys of offices overlook a striking, fully glazed entrance which half engulfs Truman's 18th-century Brewer's House and tucks neatly into other existing buildings. The stepped section is slightly top heavy over the entrance, now missing its original canopy, but this is otherwise a confident and impressive modern infill. The architects' intention to form a new urban square as part of the scheme is spoilt both by the building's relationship to the street and by a solid set of railings.

North

BARNSBURY MEWS HOUSING, Lofting Road, London N1. *Kenneth Pring and Associates.* 1974-76.

Award: DoE Good Design in Housing Award 1976.

≩ Caledonian Road or Highbury and Islington ⊖ Angel or Highbury and Islington

Cited as "one of the chief experiments of housing of the 70s", this scheme was commended by the award assessors for achieving maximum density for low rise dwellings. A mixture of flats, maisonettes and terraced houses, it manages 176 ppa, while the low massing respects neighbouring buildings within the Barnsbury Conservation Area. The scheme incorporates a network of pedestrian routes and central spine access road. Tenants were involved in the landscaping and the development has maintained its integrity while allowing residents to make their own additions.

North

CLISSOLD PARK COMPREHENSIVE SCHOOL, Clissold Road, N16. *Stillman and Eastwick-Field.* 1969.

⊖ Manor House ☎ Headmaster 01-254 0548

This ten-form entry school accommodates 1,775 pupils. Apart from classroom and the usual facilities, there are houserooms, a youth service headquarters and a further education department. A sports and drama hall obviates the need for a formal assembly area. The light brown load-bearing brickwork contrasts well with large white concrete sill beams. Vertical emphasis is given by the mullions of the glazed stair well, while the building's horizontality is reinforced by black-painted timber windows. The low, three-storey massing around brick-paved courtyards is intended to create a "collegiate" feel.

94

95

96

97

North

HIGHGATE NEW TOWN HOUSING, STAGE 2 SITE C, Dartmouth Park Hill, Highgate, N19. *London Borough of Camden Architect's Department.* 1981.
Award: Architectural Design Project Award Commendation 1981.
⊖ Archway

The final stage in the New Town development, this mixed scheme seeks to "invest each group of flats with the quality of entrance and place commonly found in the villas of the 19th century". Gestures such as the use of polychrome brickwork and arched windows pay lip service to the Victorian ideas. But the effect is over done, with a curiously extravagant use of ironmongery, the design of which seems confused. Glazed canopies over staircases on the upper level contribute further to the confusion.

North

MARQUESS ROAD HOUSING ESTATE PHASES I AND II, Essex and St Pauls Roads, N1. *Darbourne and Darke.* 1978.
Award: Phase 1: Highly Commended, DoE Good Design in Housing Award 1975.
🚌 30, 38, 73, 171 ⇌ Highbury and Islington or Essex Road ⊖ Highbury and Islington

One of the more successful attempts at relatively high density in a low rise development, this scheme manages 136 ppa, with 60 per cent family housing and 40 per cent one-bedroom flats. Social and shopping facilities are also included. A system of 5.25 m bays was established with family units on the ground floor and flats above, which allowed an atmosphere of "house dwelling" and for a large private outdoor space.

North West

BRANCH HILL HOUSING, Spedan Close, Branch Hill, NW3. *London Borough of Camden Department of Architecture.* 1978.
⊖ Hampstead

This purist exercise for Camden by Benson and Forsyth is council housing, but because of its high quality and salubrious location it could be taken for an up-market private development. Straight rows of two-storey houses are set close together along the steeply sloping site, the flat roofs of one row becoming the gardens for the row above. The plan is dense and rigid with narrow flights of steps threaded through the complex cubic forms. Inside the planning is unconventional, recalling the experimental housing of the 20s and 30s. Benson and Forsyth's Modernism is nothing if not thorough. The high cost of the scheme won it the title of the most expensive council housing in the country.

North West

TV–AM BUILDING, Hawley Crescent, NW1, *Terry Farrell Partnership.* 1983.
⊖ Camden Town ☎ Public Relations Officer 01-267 4300

The studios themselves are new structures, but the rest of this entertaining building is a converted car repair workshop on the Grand Union Canal. Farrell has taken this rather unpromising raw material and turned it into a Post-modernist manifesto. An existing long, narrow, sunken area in the middle of the building contains a Japanese temple (hospitality room) in the east, a ziggurat (staircase) in the middle east, a Venetian bridge in the west and a mirror-glass screen (dubbed the Houston screen) in the far west. Reactions to the building range from delighted enthusiasm to downright annoyance.

98

99

100

101

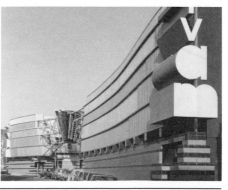

North West
CO-OWNERSHIP FLATS, 125 Park Road, NW8. *Farrell Grimshaw Partnership*. 1970.
⊖ Baker Street or St John's Wood

This simple tower looks like an office block, but contains housing society flats. Each of the roughly square floors has a central core of lifts, staircases, bathrooms and ducts. Around this a band of unobtrusive space can be partitioned off to form different configurations of units, ranging from 14 bed-sitters to four two-bedroomed flats. The flexible plan, rounded corners and lightweight metal cladding were a trademark of this practice.

North West
ELEPHANT AND RHINOCEROS PAVILION, The Zoological Gardens, Regent's Park, NW1. *Casson Conder Partnership*. 1964.
Awards: RIBA Award 1966; Civic Trust Commendation 1967.
⊖ Regent's Park or Camden Town

Resulting from the Zoo's Redevelopment Plan of 1956, this building features reinforced concrete external walls, with ribs hacked to expose the aggregate. Inside, light grey-blue mosaic faces a brick skin. The central webbed roof has laminated wood beams spanning from the perimeter to a cluster of laminated columns around the flue and air intake. The design is functional: external curved plinths and ribbed walls prevent marking and the curved plan makes internal cleaning easy. The main design source was the pen arrangement, each unit housing two pairs of animals and a sick bay arranged around an interchange lobby.

North West
HOUSING, 2c Belsize Park Gardens, NW3. *Spence and Webster*. 1981.
⊖ Belsize Park ☎ 01-267 7676

In a street of large stuccoed houses, this building is easily missed. Hidden behind a white painted wall, it was designed by Spence and Webster for their own use. Originally the planners required a building to match the scale of its neighbours, but the architects were committed to single storey living. Arguing that the site was historically a garden and the mature trees behind were a visual asset, they suggested making the building virtually invisible. With its light steel frame, extensive glazing and metal decking, the building is pure hi-tech, owing something to Michael Hopkins' house (qv) in nearby Hampstead.

North West
HOUSING, ALEXANDRA ROAD, NW8. *London Borough of Camden Department of Architecture, Neave Brown*. 1977. HOUSING FOR THE HANDICAPPED, 48 Boundary Road, NW8. *Evans and Shalev*. 1978.
Awards: Forticrete Award 1979; RIBA Commendation 1980.
⊖ Swiss Cottage

The Evans and Shalev scheme sits at the end of this dramatic crescent of public housing. Alexandra Road may be seen as the apogee of the career of the local authority housing architect – while it was still under construction comprehensive redevelopment had given way to refurbishment and piecemeal building. The housing has been criticised for its cost and its heating system, but its biggest problem is a mismatch of tenants' aspirations and architects' dreams. As a composition, it is a dramatic and successful piece of townscape.

102

103

104

105

North West
HUMANA HOSPITAL WELLINGTON, Wellington Road, NW8. *YRM Partnership* 1978-1982.
⊖ St John's Wood ☏ Hospital Administrator 01-586 5959
    The hospital has two buildings in the same block. The southernmost, completed in 1978, has a simple linear stepped form which belies the complexity of the internal plan. The steps form the wards, while treatment areas, operating theatres and so on occupy the lower floors and internal spaces. The second building, completed in 1982, has a stepped profile on the west side only, but it has the same smooth stone cladding and large flush windows. This is mainstream Modernism at its most severe – a style not inappropriate for this busy London thoroughfare.

North West
MAIDEN LANE HOUSING, off Agar Grove, NW1. *London Borough of Camden Department of Architecture.* 1979-82.
Awards: Architectural Design Bronze Medal 1983.
⊖ Camden Town
    Benson and Forsyth's housing scheme for Camden makes no concessions to contemporary fashion. The rigid rectilinear plan, cubic forms, dramatic cantilevered slabs and white painted concrete recall the pioneering pre-war housing of Frankfurt or Stuttgart. The black and white colour scheme is relieved only by red brick paving and touches of red and green in the metal balustrades. There is not a brick wall or pitched roof in sight. This development is a far cry from the shoddy grey concrete monstrosities that gave Modernism a bad name.

North West
MEWS HOUSE AND STUDIO, 22 Murray Mews, Camden, NW1. *Tom Kay.* 1971.
Awards: Civic Trust Commendation 1973; Eternit International Prize for Architecture 1974; Architectural Heritage Year Commendation 1975.
⇌ Camden Road ⊖ Camden Town ☏ Tom Kay 01-267 2645
    Kay's house is an outstanding example of innovative design using traditional materials in a fairly mixed context. Set between a 1967 brick house and a rendered Victorian coach house, the building seeks to complement the one while providing a transition to the other. The *Architectural Review* of July 1975 said: "The result is a house that is superbly integrated into its urban surroundings. . . . Every opportunity has been taken to maximise space, light and volume and levels on a small site, and the result is a truly innovative house".

North West
MICHAEL HOPKINS HOUSE, 2 Downshire Hill, NW3. *Michael Hopkins.* 1977.
Awards: RIBA Award 1977; Civic Trust Award 1977.
⊖ Hampstead ☏ Michael Hopkins 01-435 1109
    From the outside the house appears to be constructed of large sheets of glass and very little else: inside the short structural spans give the steel frame a super-lightweight, almost flimsy look. The plan is extremely simple: two rectangular floors, linked by a central spiral staircase, with no permanent partitioning except to bathrooms and stores. The street entrance is at first floor level. Stylistically the house could not be more remote from its Regency neighbours, but it fits into the street surprisingly well.

106

107

108

109

North West
ROYAL COLLEGE OF PHYSICIANS, St Andrew's Place, Regent's Park, London NW1. *Denys Lasdun & Partners.* 1960.
Awards: RIBA Bronze Medal 1964; Civic Trust Award 1967.
⊖ Regent's Park ☏ 01-935 1174

The Royal College replaced Nash's war-damaged Someries House, and sits comfortably adjacent to a preserved Nash terrace, part of which is being refurbished by the College. The structure is mainly reinforced concrete. The two-storey library, floating over the foyer, has in-situ, pre-stressed concrete units supported only by central free-standing columns and an internal cross-wall. The main roof is of pre-cast concrete slabs on steel castellated beams. The brick walled lecture theatre, with its sloping walls, has a steel pyramidal space frame roof.

North West
SNOWDON AVIARY, London Zoo, Regent's Park, NW1. *Lord Snowdon, Cedric Price and Frank Newby.* 1963.
🚌 4, 3, 53 ⊖ Regent's Park

This unusual structure was commissioned by the Zoological Society in 1960. Lord Snowdon was asked to design a large "walk through" aviary between the Regent's Canal (from which it may be viewed with advantage) and Prince Albert Road. Lord Snowdon asked Cedric Price to collaborate with him and, together, they invited the engineer Frank Newby to act as consultant. The team came up with a design which features two crystalline end pavilions connected by a net running over tension cables.

North West
TOLMERS SQUARE OFFICES AND HOUSING, 250 Euston Road, NW1. *Renton Howard Wood Levin Partnership.* 1981.
⊖ Warren Street or Euston Square

This mixed development replacing a fine Georgian Square has two distinct styles. The brick-clad housing is arranged around a new informal square which, despite the high density and proximity to one of London's busiest roads, has a quiet residential character. The office block is quite another matter. Its façade is completely cloaked in mirror glass, with shiny stainless steel mullions and transoms, applied to a complicated building form.

South East
HORNIMAN PRIMARY SCHOOL, Horniman Drive, Forest Hill, SE23. *Michael Manser Associates.* 1971.
Award: Civic Trust Commendation 1973.
🚌 P4 from Brixton to Honor Oak Road ⇌ Forest Hill

Set on an awkward sloping site, only the low plastic clad administrative blocks are visible from the street. Behind on lower ground is the main steel-framed building with classrooms, double height hall, and cloakrooms. Its ingenious layout gives it an appropriately small scale and disguises its true size from passers-by. The school has worn well, apart from inevitable leaking through the flat roof.

110

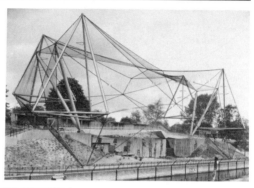

111

112

113

South East
LAKESIDE HEALTH CENTRE, Tavybridge, Thamesmead, SE2. *Derek Slow and Partners*. 1972, extension 1982.
➤ Abbey Wood

Easily the best early Thamesmead building, the health centre is basically of steel and glass on a concrete deck, contrasting with the surrounding pre-cast concrete buildings. From the shopping precinct it appears single storey, the diagonal cut-offs between wall and roof providing an elegant human scale. From the east it appears stilted, rising on two legs from the lake to create an exciting piece of townscape. It works and has worn well, though maintenance seems less than adequate.

South East
MODERN ART GLASS FACTORY, Hailey Road, Thamesmead Eastern Industrial Estate, Erith, Kent. *Foster Associates*. 1973.
Award: Financial Times Industrial Architecture Award 1974.
➤ Belvedere

Now surrounded by sheds, this is the only building of architectural note on the industrial estate. The curved envelope embracing roof and walls and glazed end wall is a forerunner of the Sainsbury Centre, and shows what good visual design can make of a basic industrial building. Though much imitated by public sector factory designers, here the building stands in a class of its own. Sadly, the planners have not encouraged others to design such good looking factories.

South East
MORLEY COLLEGE EXTENSIONS, 61 Westminster Bridge Road and 1-13 King Edward Walk, SE1. *John Winter and Associates*. 1973 and 1983.
⊖ Lambeth North ☎ 01-928 8501

There is more than a hint of Mies in the first of Winter's extensions. Set behind the unprepossessing main block, the sleek brown metal-clad block has dark glazed horizontal banding. Inside, the reinforced concrete structure is revealed in the teaching rooms and studios. By contrast, the latest addition is a cheerfully bright shed in corrugated Cor-Ten weathering steel with bright yellow paintwork. Presenting a linear face to the road, the building fans out at the back under the cascading Cor-Ten roof.

South East
SOUTH BANK ARTS COMPLEX, Waterloo, SE1. *Various architects*. 1951 onwards.
Awards: Royal Festival Hall Extension (London County Council Architects) Civic Trust Award 1967; Queen Elizabeth Hall (GLC Architects) Civic Trust Award 1970.
➤ Waterloo or Charing Cross ⊖ Waterloo or Embankment

The 1951 Festival of Britain gave a massive boost to the post-war design culture. The South Bank Arts Centre masterminded by the then London County Council, is its permanent reincarnation. Its main monuments are the Royal Festival Hall, designed under Sir Leslie Martin in 1951, and extended towards the river in 1963 under Sir Hubert Bennett; and Bennett's Hayward Gallery and Queen Elizabeth Hall opened in 1967/68. The National Theatre, designed by Sir Denys Lasdun and Partners, was completed in 1977.

114

115

116

117

South East
TRAFALGAR ESTATE HOUSING, 8-26 Trafalgar Road and Corvette Square, SE10. *James Gowan and Julian Blades.* 1968.
⇌ Maze Hill

A low-key, but well considered and witty response to the Royal Naval College opposite, this scheme is enlightened for its time. Four linked four-storey blocks arranged around a courtyard have a brick skin which is plain to the point of puritanism with nautical touches in windows, railings and funnel-like refuse chutes. Each unit has a balcony or small walled garden and despite the relatively high density the scheme seems to work and is well maintained.

South West
BP HOUSE/ASHDOWN HOUSE, Victoria Street SW1. *Elsom Pack and Roberts.* 1975.
⇌ Victoria ⊖ Victoria

Victoria Street is an extraordinary canyon with slab office blocks on the north side and this very different development on the other. To expose the Byzantine Westminster Cathedral set to the south, the offices are heaped like building blocks to the east and west, stepping down to a break point towards the western end. It is a simple device of massing rather than a stylistic tour de force, but it serves well enough, giving this colossal street a clear design intention.

South West
CHURCHILL GARDENS, Pimlico, SW1. *Powell & Moya.* 1946–1962.
Awards: RIBA Bronze Medal for Architecture 1950; Civic Trust Award 1961.
⊖ Pimlico

The estate is the result of a competition which established the practice of Powell and Moya. It has proved to be an enormously successful scheme, well liked by residents and well maintained by Westminster City Council. It was originally heated by a district scheme using waste heat from the Battersea Power Station across the river; since the station closed down it has had its own boiler system.

South West
CLORE BUILDING, TATE GALLERY, Millbank, SW1. *James Stirling, Michael Wilford and Associates.*
⊖ Westminster or Pimlico

Seen by some as the definitive Post-modernist statement or as a piece of frippery, this is, in fact, what Stirling describes as "an architectural conversation". A mixed bag of styles is used to create the permanent home for the Clore Bequest's Turner collection. A Classical stone façade complements the Tate, but the stone panels give way to brick as they approach the adjacent Edwardian military hospital. Disparate elements are clamped together to form a building that makes a virtue out of contextualism.

118

119

120

121

South West
CROWN REACH, Grosvenor Road, SW1. *Nicholas Lacey and Associates.*
1983.
⊖ Pimlico
    The form of this competition-winning scheme arises from the requirement not to obstruct river views of other Crown Estate properties and to give maximum views of the river to the tenants of the luxurious flats. The vast, sloping lead roofs provide a dramatic, if rather bleak view to the rear while the broken, ziggurat river frontage is delicately handled and, despite difficulties in construction, faithful to the original design.

South West
DANISH EMBASSY, 55 Sloane Street, SW1. *Arne Jacobsen.* 1977.
⊖ Knightsbridge or Sloane Square
    Although very much a 60s design with its dark grey concrete cladding, brown tinted glazing and turgid green-painted aluminium shades, Jacobsen's last building is low key, echoing the proportions of the surrounding Edwardian terraces. The vertical elements below the parapet are emphasised by setting back the two glazed upper floors and at street level the cladding is sculpted. The gardens opposite in Cadogan Place give the Embassy room to breathe, but from the back its bulk is more evident and it dwarfs the mews houses of Hans Crescent.

South West
ECONOMIST BUILDING, 25 St James's Street, SW1. *Alison and Peter Smithson.* 1964.
⊖ Green Park ☎ 01-839 7000
    One of the Smithson's few commercial commissions, this development slots comfortably into fashionable St James's and raises few eyebrows nowadays. The little plaza from which the bocks rise is of rather smaller scale than we have come to expect from similar city developments. Stone detailing to the mullions and somewhat spindly piloti has weathered and blackened in places. Good open access from plaza level creates an ambulatory effect and serves to lighten the building's bulk at eye level. These days this is an interesting rather than a fascinating development, pleasing more for its human scale than for architectural bravura.

South West
HOUSING, ALTON ESTATE, Roehampton Lane, SW15. *LCC Architect's Department.* 1955 (West), 1959 (East).
⇌ Barnes
    Built during the heyday of the LCC Architect's Department when it was full of committed young architects, the Estate was developed in two phases. The West Estate is designed with a distinctly Scandinavian influence while the East Estate is a Unité look-alike. However the blocks fail to operate in the solid groups that Le Corbusier intended.

122

123

124

125

South West

HOUSEHOLD CAVALRY REGIMENT BARRACKS, Knightsbridge, SW7. *Sir Basil Spence, Anthony Blee and John Dangerfield.* 1970.

⊖ Knightsbridge ☎ Camp Commandant 01-930 4466

Occupying a long narrow site between Knightsbridge and Hyde Park, the barracks complex is dominated by its least attractive feature – a 28-storey concrete faced residential tower which intrudes into views of the park. The rest of the development attempts to temper human scale brick faced flats and offices to the needs of the barracks and the importance of security. The complex is broken down into small blocks to reduce its impact and the long brick perimeter wall is staggered to break its monotony. Apart from accommodation, the barracks includes social and sports facilities, stables and riding school.

South West

LILLINGTON GARDENS HOUSING, Lillington Street, SW1. *Darbourne and Darke.* 1972.

Awards: Housing Design Award 1961; Ministry of Housing and Local Government Award for Good Design 1970; RIBA Award 1970; RIBA Commendation 1973.

⇌ Victoria ⊖ Victoria or Pimlico

With some 780 dwellings, this is one of the last of London's high-density public housing schemes and one of the most distinguished. Four blocks form an enclosing wall round the site with wings pushing into its interior. Enclosed gardens compare with the squares of nearby Pimlico while pedestrian areas give views of St James-the-Less church. The structure is in-situ beams and slabs with load-bearing brick cross walls. Hand made multi-red brick facings have raked joints and windows are timber.

South West

MILLBANK TOWER, formerly called Vickers House, Millbank, SW1. *Ronald Ward and Partners.* 1963.

⊖ Pimlico or Westminster then 77 or 88 bus

One of the earliest towers to be built in London it is one of the most elegant. Its prominent siting remains successful because it has not attracted any neighbours of similar bulk. The curved curtain wall façade reinforces the building's relationship with the river, reflecting the bend between Vauxhall and Lambeth which it marks.

South West

METROPOLITAN POLICE OFFICE, 1 Drummond Gate, SW1. *Chapman Taylor Partners.* 1983.

⊖ Pimlico

In stark contrast to the revivalist character of the Whitfield design next door, this building provides an elegant mixture of polished commercial development and fashionable high-tech. Chapman Taylor have designed the master plan for the Millbank Estate owned by the Crown Estate Commissioners and covering some 27 acres at the north end of Vauxhall Bridge. The focus of their plan is Bessborough Gardens which includes an ornamental fountain designed by Sir Peter Shepheard.

126

127

128

129

South West
METROPOLITAN POLICE OFFICE, Rampayne St, SW1. *Whitfield Partners.* 1982.
⊖ Pimlico
   William Whitfield is the master of contextualism and is frequently hired as a consultant in 'tricky' historic areas to produce architecture that fits in with its neighbours. The choice of this Victorian warehouse aesthetic on a site between Lillington Gardens and Chapman Taylor's high-tech design next door is a curious one. The resultant building is bulky and the mansard top hat inelegant.

South West
NATURAL HISTORY MUSEUM EXTENSION, Cromwell Road, SW7. *John Pinckheard.* 1975.
⊖ South Kensington ☎ Palaeontology reception 01-589 6323
   The four floors of the new extension are concealed behind dark glazing broken into large "windows" by the curved concrete structure. The end wing, with its lacy concrete crown, adds height and draws the building towards Waterhouse's original Museum. Though the new block harmonises well with the old while making its own strong statement, the concrete has discoloured and does not compare well with the blond and blue brickwork of the Waterhouse building. Less successful is the side elevation where the extension is linked to the Geological Museum by a blank concrete slab above large metalled doors.

South West
NEW COVENT GARDEN MARKET, 1 Nine Elms Lane, SW8. *GMW Partnership.* 1975.
Award: Commendation in the Financial Times Industrial Architecture Award for the Flower Market Roof Structure 1975.
⇌ Vauxhall ⊖ Vauxhall
   When it opened this complex was described as "a machine for selling, a product of rational 60s thinking which adds nothing to the life and fabric of the city". The twin administrative slab blocks rising 21 and 16 storeys from their podium are linked to the Flower Market by a high level glazed bridge. The most interesting feature is the flower market, a giant cream coloured egg box of glass reinforced polyester set above offices. The fruit and vegetable market has two grey metal clad parallel blocks linked by two bridges.

South West
PIMLICO SCHOOL, Lupus Street, SW1. *GLC Architect's Department.* 1970.
Awards: RIBA Award 1972; Civic Trust Award 1973.
⊖ Pimlico
   It is a tour de force in concrete and patent glazing imposing a strong but alien form on Cubitt's Pimlico. The school is a large scale urban comprehensive known particularly for its work in environmental design, perhaps inspired by the building. The building has not been well maintained, and high solar gain has forced occupants to employ untidy temporary control systems.

130

131

132

133

South West
ROYAL COLLEGE OF ART, Kensington Gore, SW7. *H. T. Cadbury-Brown with Sir Hugh Casson.* 1962.
⊖ South Kensington, High Street Kensington

A big, brown elephant of a building that was intended to match the Norman Shaw blocks nearby; but the dark bricks and mullions bear little relationship to the light Victorian touch. The tall windows in the top floors say "studio", but there is little else to distinguish it from an expensive office block – even the low level exhibition areas at the entrance have been simply treated in contrast to Denys Lasdun's Royal College of Physicians, where the lecture hall provided relief from the formal grids.

South West
WORLDS END HOUSING DEVELOPMENT, Cheyne Walk, SW10. *Eric Lyons, Cadbury-Brown, Metcalfe and Cunningham.* 1977.
⊖ Fulham Broadway

When opened, this development was described as a "courageous attempt at overcoming the apparently intractable problems of high rise, high density housing". But its success is limited. The warm brickwork of the clustered towers has weathered well. The blocks are made visually interesting by their sculpted tops and the façades broken by angled balconies. But the complex is still oppressive and overwhelming. Vandalism has not been prevented; it is evident that the problems are indeed intractable and that there is a limit to what designers can do to solve social problems.

West
HOUSING, 103-123 St Marks Road, W10. *Jeremy Dixon.* 1979.
⊖ Ladbroke Grove

Now considered a classic scheme, St Marks Road clearly indicates Dixon's streetscape thinking. Drawing references from the surrounding architecture, he has meticulously interpreted features such as the raised entrances, porches and pitched gables, almost exaggerating them to make them his own. Materials are carefully selected to provide a built-in richness to the design. The result is a terrace that is deliberately "all front". Behind the façade the "backs" adopt a lower but equally well considered status in keeping with their neighbours.

West
KENSINGTON TOWN HALL AND LIBRARY, Hornton Street, W8. *John S. Bonnington Partnership.* 1977.
⊖ High Street Kensington ☎ 01-937 5464

Though not outwardly typical with its varied brick façades and human scale this building reflects grandiose 60s thinking in civic terms. The large civic suite has its own entrance and the free-standing council chamber on four cruciform concrete columns is nothing short of opulent inside. Despite the efforts at human scale, the building appears too big for the site shared with the library completed in 1960. The internal courtyard seems oppressive with little concession to greenery and the entry points are dark and uninviting.

134

135

136

137

West

PHILLIPS WEST TWO, 10 Salem Road, W2. *Campbell Zogolovitch Wilkinson and Gough* 1976.

⊖ Bayswater ☎ Local manager 01-221 5303

This is a wonderfully whimsical transformation of a warehouse into auction rooms, with housing above and offices behind. The architects have added an extra storey to the T-shaped block creating an internal landscaped courtyard overlooked by the houses and offices. The entire complex is painted pink with a bulbous balcony of navy blue flat metal straps bent to shape. The metalwork curves up to the roof and loops downwards to the striking entrance with its jazzy blue neon sign. Inside are two auction rooms in pale green with navy blue timber.

Middlesex

HEINZ RESEARCH AND ADMINISTRATION CENTRE, Hayes Park, Hayes, Middx. *Skidmore Owings and Merrill with Matthews Ryan and Partners.* 1965.

Award: Civic Trust Award 1967.

🚃 A40 to Hayesend ⇌ Hayes and Harlington ☎ 01-573 7757

Great effort was taken here to produce a fine building of its time. A typical American parkland design, the result still looks as trim 20 years on as it did on completion. This is largely due to the quality of the workmanship and Heinz's fastidious maintenance habits. The façades are disappointing and rather fussy; the waisted columns take away some of the sharpness necessary to provide a satisfactory contrast between building and landscape.

Middlesex

HILLINGDON CIVIC CENTRE, High Street, Uxbridge, Middx. *Robert Matthew Johnson-Marshall and Partners.* 1976-78.

⊖ Uxbridge ☎ 0895 50111

The first major building of the 70s vernacular revival, this was a brave attempt to humanise the town hall. It is fascinating lesson in the anachronisms produced by designers attempting to revive architectural styles inappropriate to a building type and method. The evidence of the brick veneer is in stark contrast to the solidity the style tries to communicate; the image of an oversized semi-detached house presents an interesting relationship between the town hall and its suburban domain. But the building has much popular appeal in a borough plagued more than most by 60s systemised housing failures.

Middlesex

McKAY TRADING ESTATE, Blackthorne Road, Poyle, Middx. *John Outram Architects.* 1978.

🚃 M4, then A4 and Bath Road ⊖ Heathrow

Definitely up market, this scheme takes the industrial shed and lifts it to a higher plane to create an urbane environment. The façade features double height brick arches to accommodate the large entrance door with two-storey offices fronting the industrial space. The access yard has become a spacious piazza. Outram draws references from Louis Kahn "to set up a dialogue between appearance and reality" and "release the imagination from its imprisonment within the suffocating materialism of contemporary modern architecture". Be that as it may, this is quite a remarkable building lovingly detailed.

138

139

140

141

Northern

Chester-le-Street
CIVIC CENTRE, Newcastle Road, Chester-le-Street, Co Durham. *Faulkner-Brown Hendy Watkinson Stonor*. 1982.
≥ Chester-le-Street ☎ Chief Technical Officer 0385 882521
   This dramatic silver building has been cleverly sited as a landmark in the Victorian tradition of civic pride. The gently sloping site is exploited to create three different spaces for council, amenity and administrative functions. The whole is drawn together by the barrel vaulted mall which provides the spine and helps to create a light, airy interior.

Darlington
CUMMINS ENGINEERING FACTORY, Yarm Road, Darlington, Co Durham. *Kevin Roche, John Dinkeloo and Associates*. 1960.
🚍 A67 🚍 80 from Darlington ≥ Darlington ☎ 0325 6060
   This factory is a classic temple of steel and glass containing broad flexible spaces. The first use of Cor-Ten weathering steel in Britain, the structure comprises steel H-sections built up from a brick stylobate fully exploiting the Classical grammar of colonnades, capitals and entablature. Another first is the use on this scale of structural Neoprene gaskets to frame the full height grey-tinted glazing and the consistent use of these materials for internal partitioning.

Durham
COLLINGWOOD COLLEGE, University of Durham, Stone Road, Durham. *Sheppard Robson*. 1974.
Award: RIBA Award 1974.
≥ Durham 🚍 X20, 214 ☎ 0385 67121
   A steeply sloping site and fine mature trees influenced the design of this building. Study bedrooms step down the slope in two wings, each comprising a series of interconnecting blocks served by their own staircases from a common access gallery. The gallery is at the same level as the communal block, which houses dining and administrative facilities, the library and the main entrance. The ground falls away from the communal block forming a lower level for the junior common room and recreational facilities. The building is largely of loadbearing brick on block construction.

142

143

144

Durham
DUNELM HOUSE STUDENT RECREATION CENTRE, University of Durham, New Elvet, Durham. *Architects Co-Partnership.* 1967.
Awards: RIBA Award 1967; Civic Trust Award 1968.
≈ Durham

Built mainly in lightweight concrete, this building occupies a dramatic site on a steep river bank. The design shows how a concrete building can resemble sculpture, with a series of in-situ reinforced concrete boxes tucked into the bank. Lightweight concrete is used for the walls to provide excellent thermal insulation. The delightful Kingsgate Bridge in the foreground, designed by Sir Ove Arup, is a fine example of slender concrete construction pared down to its essentials.

Durham
MILBURNGATE SHOPPING CENTRE, Durham. *Building Design Partnership.* 1976.
Awards: RIBA Commendation 1977; Civic Trust Award 1978; Europa Nostra Medal 1978.
≈ Durham

This scheme provides 17,000 sq m of shopping and car parking space, while remaining sympathetic in scale and quality to the old town. Pitched slate roofs, modelled buff bricks and careful planning help to mask its true size. Assessors awarding the RIBA Commendation said the scheme "is a model of self-effacing modesty. Its ambition is to achieve a modern vernacular which merges the city with the houses and shops around, forming part of the continuous backdrop the town as a whole provides to the very dramatic centre, cathedral and river."

Falstone
KIELDER WATER, KIELDER RESERVOIR, Falstone, Upper Tyne Valley, Northumbria. *Frederick Gibberd & Partners.* 1982.
A696 from Newcastle to Otterburn, B6320 to Bellingham, then C200 to Falstone or C200 south east from Kielder Castle.

This reservoir is Europe's largest man-made lake, lying in the heart of a man-made forest, providing many leisure facilities. The earth dam just above the village creates a reservoir 9.6 km long with a shoreline of nearly 45 km. The primary design objective was to reconcile the new engineering works with the landscape and to exploit the visual opportunities offered by a vast sheet of water in a magnificent landscape setting.

Harriston
HARRISTON VILLAGE HOUSING, Nr Aspatria, Allerdale, Cumbria. *Napper Collerton Partnership.* 1977.
Awards: DoE Housing Design Award 1978; Concrete Society Award 1980; RIBA Commendation 1980; Civic Trust Award 1980.
off A596 ≈ Aspatria

This project was part of the rebuilding of an old mining village in a programme phased to keep the existing community intact. The design was based on the character of that community, the nature of the site and the original village structure. Though the initial objective was not to design the clichéd English village, an appreciation of these factors involved dovetailing existing restrictions with future potential and resulted in a form which is obviously part of a continuing village tradition.

145

146

147

148

Newcastle upon Tyne
BLACKFRIARS, Friars Street, Newcastle upon Tyne. *Wales, Wales, and Rawson.* 1980.
Awards: Civic Trust Award, 1981; Silver Award, Formica European Design Competition 1981.
≈ Newcastle upon Tyne Ⓜ St James 🚌 From Newgate Street ☎ 0632 615367

This fine 13th-century Dominican friary has been restored as a tourist centre. Located within the old city walls, the building is of unique architectural significance. The restoration of window and door openings, stonework and roofing has been complemented by a corner addition of brickwork sympathetic to the stone but distinct from it.

Newcastle upon Tyne
BRITISH GAS ENGINEERING RESEARCH STATION, Northumbrian Way, Killingworth, Newcastle upon Tyne. *Ryder and Yates and Partners.* 1969.
Awards: Concrete Society Commendation 1968; RIBA Award 1969; Civic Trust Award 1969.
≈ Newcastle Ⓜ Killingworth ☎ 0632 684828

The brief called for a flexible and extendable building. The design incorporates a fixed element containing offices and catering facilities with an extendable space for laboratories and workshop. White concrete Venturi-style towers, cylindrical water turrets, entrance bridge and triangular gateway pylons add interest to the modular precast concrete panel-clad exterior. The building has been described as "a remarkable chameleon. Everything that could possibly be movable is movable and is constantly changing to meet the research requirements."

Newcastle upon Tyne
BYKER HOUSING REDEVELOPMENT, Newcastle upon Tyne, *Ralph Erskine Architect Planner AB.*
Awards: Ambrose Congreve Award 1979; Civic Trust Award 1979; Eternit Award 1980.
≈ Newcastle upon Tyne Ⓜ Byker

Described by Andrew Saint in the *New Statesman* as "the most spectacular and unequivocally successful British housing development of recent times", this redevelopment sought to retain the existing community while involving residents in the development of the scheme. The various phases have their own style, each becoming more confidently idiosyncratic. The generous sweeps of the famous wall enclosing small terraces tumbling down the hill produce an exuberance of colour and form and the more the skilful landscape matures, the more enchanting the spaces become.

Newcastle upon Tyne
CLAYTON STREET WEST DEVELOPMENT, Newcastle upon Tyne. *Barnett Curry Smith.* 1982.
≈ Newcastle Ⓜ Central ☎ 0632 328821

An important feature of this scheme is that it re-introduces residential units to the city centre. In all there are 260 homes, largely for single people or childless couples, with offices and shops built into the lower floors. Along one side of the development, two-storey galleried apartments are set behind a retained façade and the architects have shown sympathy for the original in their choice of style and materials. At the heart of the development is a green space with raised lawn, tennis court and trees.

149

150

151

152

Newcastle upon Tyne
ELSWICK SWIMMING POOL AND PARK, Beech Grove Road, Elswick,
Newcastle upon Tyne. *Napper Collerton Partnership.* 1980.
≉ Newcastle upon Tyne Ⓜ Central ☎ 0632 737801

Originally the grounds of the Georgian Elswick Hall, the park has been
restored for recreational use. The pool acts as the architectural focus and
is designed in the English winter garden tradition. A freely expressed steel
lattice structure supports profiled metal cladding and a glazed roof. The
changing pavilion, by contrast, uses brick and dark stained timber to blend
with the surroundings and has a low, curved, copper-clad roof. It acts as a
buffer between the potentially noisy sports areas and the more sedate
bowling greens.

Newcastle upon Tyne
MEA HOUSE, Ellison Place, Newcastle upon Tyne. *Ryder and Yates and
Partners.* 1978.
Award: RIBA Commendation 1978.
≉ Newcastle upon Tyne Ⓜ Central ☎ 0632 327783

This was the first British project to house a range of voluntary organisa-
tions under one roof. Cool clarity of thought is evident in the planning and
apparent ease with which the elevations rise around an unusually sophisticated structure. Dominating the façade are two great glazed walls. The
grey, lightly-mirrored glass diminishes solar gain while unifying Ellison
Place.

Newcastle upon Tyne
METRO RAPID TRANSIT SYSTEM, Newcastle upon Tyne. *Consultant
architects: Faulkner-Brown, Hendy, Watkinson, Stonor. Executive architects: Waring and Netts Partnership, L.J. Couves and Partners and Ainsworth Spark Associates.* 1983.
≉ Newcastle upon Tyne ☎ 0632 610431

The design concept for the stations on the Metro system, defined as
glass and steel, is based on a kit of parts which creates a strong visual identity throughout the system. So far it has been successful in resisting vandalism. Stations are restrained, each responding differently to its setting,
but with a consistency of detail and bright colours to provide lively interiors.
Several on the Coast Line are restored Victorian structures, and
Tynemouth in particular recalls the splendour of the bygone steam age.

Newcastle upon Tyne
NEWCASTLE AIRPORT, Woolsington, Newcastle upon Tyne. *YRM Archi-
tects and Planners.* 1967, extension 1982.
Award: RIBA Bronze Medal 1968.
✈ A696 Ⓜ Bunk Foot ☎ Deputy Director (Operations) 0632 860966

Designed to handle some 650 passengers an hour, the terminal building
is a reinforced concrete structure with white tiled cladding. The extension
aims to preserve the architectural quality of the existing complex by incorporating the same form and materials; but one new feature, the elevated
pier with steel frame and light aluminium cladding, has been designed to
express its own identity.

153

154

155

156

Redcar
PUBLIC LIBRARY, Goatham Road, Redcar, Yorkshire. *Ahrends Burton and Koralek.* 1971.
⇒ Redcar

Sited within a group of other social facilities, this library has a deliberately uninstitutional character and welcoming open plan. Wide span and largely single storey, the building features top-lit spaces. Steel columns support castellated beams with a folded roof providing continuous roof lights. Inside the planning is geared to efficiency, with quiet areas on the upper level and a specially designed children's library. A coffee bar and exhibition area are incorporated into the entrance and there is an interesting winter garden.

Sunderland
TOWN HALL AND CIVIC CENTRE, West Park, Sunderland. *Sir Basil Spence, Bonnington and Collins.* 1970.
Awards: RIBA Award 1971; Civic Trust Award 1972.
⇒ Sunderland ☎ 0783 76161

A hexagonal plan forming a triangular grid contains the civic suite, offices for 18 departments and a four-storey car park. The buildings follow the slope of the site, stepping back as they gain height to form terracing and courtyards overlooking the town and docks. An unobtrusive reinforced concrete structure forms low informal buildings with the car park bridging nearby railway cuttings. The complex is clad in brown brindled engineering bricks with matching tiles for walls and paving.

Washington
FATFIELD VILLAGE, District 13, Washington, Tyne and Wear. *Washington Development Corporation Architect's Department.* 1981.
Award: DoE Good Design in Housing Commendation 1978.
🚌 A1231 🚌 194, 179 or 638 from Heworth Ⓜ Heworth

One of the housing villages of Washington New Town, Fatfield comprises 532 rented homes, single person housing and a village centre. Arranged in tiers on the upper part of the River Wear valley, the development features split level homes on the steeper gradients to exploit the southern aspect and views. Pantiled roofing and rendered blockwork are the main materials. The village centre acts as a visual crown, linking the settlement in form and materials with the adjacent arts centre.

Washington
LAMBTON VILLAGE, DISTRICT 1, Washington, Tyne and Wear. *Washington Development Corporation Architect's Department.* 1982.
🚌 A1231 🚌 192, 193, 194 or 638 from Heworth Ⓜ Heworth

Now comprising 812 rented homes, Lambton will eventually include a further 300 private houses. The village is planned around an existing copse and waggonway, now forming the main walkway to the centre. Here are shops, community facilities and a pub, with the clock tower framing the focal point. A variety of forms and materials gives each dwelling its individuality and materials blend subtly with the mature environment. The road pattern features culs-de-sac shared by cars and pedestrians where the scale is reduced by dividing the width equally into concrete blocks and tarmac.

157

158

159

160

North West

Blackburn
CENTRAL AREA DEVELOPMENT, Blackburn, Lancs. *Building Design Partnership*. 1968-78.
Award: Phase 1: Civic Trust Award 1970.
≥ Blackburn
    A sparkling white jewel in the grey urban skyline, this is one of the most workable and stylish comprehensive town centre developments. A 15-storey council office block, with roof-top parking, adjoins the fine Victorian Town Hall in the pedestrian precinct. Phase I comprised 60 shops and three department stores, with phases II and III adding further shopping. Special features include two fountains within internal courtyards and landscaped open areas.

Lancaster
BATH MILL HOUSING, Dalton Road, Lancaster. *Building Design Partnership*. 1979.
Awards: DoE Good Design in Housing 1979; Civic Trust Award 1980; RIBA Commendation 1980.
≥ Lancaster
    Stone with slate roofs was preferred for this mix of four-person houses and two-person flats. But economically it did not fall within cost yardstick constraints and was successfully replaced by traditional rendered elevations. Pedestrians and traffic are separated and there are canal-side walks. The Civic Trust citation said "The commitment to simple forms and decoration is entirely justified." Sadly the Housing Association has now changed the architects' original colour scheme.

Liverpool
METROPOLITAN CATHEDRAL OF CHRIST THE KING, Brownlow Hill, Liverpool. *Frederick Gibberd and Partners*. 1967.
≥ Liverpool Lime Street
    Known locally as "Paddy's wigwam", this building has achieved the symbolism and occasional affection that befits a city landmark. Raised on a podium, concrete frames define the nave space and rise to support the conical roof and lantern tower. Externally the most dominant feature, the tower expresses the sanctuary as the most important space inside. Though it is not weathering well, which weakens its uncertain form, a view of the building has its moments of excitement and pleasure.

161

162

163

Liverpool

PLAYHOUSE THEATRE EXTENSION, Williamson Square, Liverpool. *Hall O'Donahue and Wilson.* 1968.

≥ Liverpool Lime Street ☏ 051-709 8363

The new foyer and restaurant were part of a comprehensive redevelopment of support facilities. Backstage requirements restricted the area for the new front of house, so the design features a cantilevered upper level extending beyond the building line. To preserve the symmetry of the existing Victorian façade, a detached form was used, consisting of interlocking circles and a transparent façade. In all, it is quite a virtuoso performance, but watch out for downdrafts off the restaurant glazing.

Liverpool

THE FESTIVAL HALL, International Garden Festival 1984, Priory Wood, Liverpool. *Arup Associates.* 1984.

≥ Lime Street, Central Station, St Michael's 🚌 Festival special from Lime Street ☏ 051 727 8000

The result of a major competition mounted by the Merseyside Development Corporation, the Festival Hall is one of the largest barrel vaulted structures in the world. It is almost 130 m long and has a clear-span width of nearly 60 m. At each end are two partial hemispheres. The main barrel vault section is based on the three-pin arch principle. Loads are carried through to the foundations via linked vertical and inclined bi-pods which are tied under the building at 6 m centres. The cladding is 20 mm twin-walled polycarbonate sheets; end sections have aluminium cladding. In 1985 the Hall will be converted, probably to a sports use.

Manchester

CHLORIDE TECHNICAL LTD RESEARCH AND DEVELOPMENT BUILDING, Wynne Avenue, Swinton, Manchester. *Building Design Partnership.* 1977.

Awards: RIBA Award 1978; Constrado Award 1979.

🚗 M62 junction 15 ☏ Operations Executive 061-793 5000

The brief for this development involved upgrading existing workshops and providing new accommodation suitable for future expansion. New workshops and offices are housed in a steel portal frame structure with composite sandwich cladding. An early example of a now familiar aesthetic, the result was described by the RIBA jury as ''a competent piece of design which looks attractive and stands out from the mediocrity of the earlier industrial buildings which surround it''.

Manchester

PALL MALL COURT OFFICES, King Street, Manchester. *Brett and Pollen in association with A.H. Brotherton and Partners.* 1968.

Awards: RIBA Award 1970; Civic Trust Award 1970.

≥ Manchester Piccadilly

The design was evolved to take advantage of a street of strong architectural character. The resulting building has highly modelled reflective surfaces to pick-up the texture and imagery of the surroundings. The RIBA jury described it as ''a first class city building . . . contributing to the urban environment by its relation to adjacent buildings and the handling of the pedestrian spaces created''. Next door is Casson and Conder's NatWest Bank.

164

165

166

167

Manchester
ROYAL EXCHANGE THEATRE, St Anne's Square, Manchester. *Levitt Bernstein in association with Richard Negri.* 1976.
Award: RIBA Award 1977.
≷ Manchester Piccadilly ☎ 061-833 9333
  This 750-seat theatre in the existing Edwardian Cotton Exchange is one of the architectural and engineering wonders of Britain. The seven-sided theatre is suspended within an exposed tubular steel structure bearing on four existing masonry piers. Seating is on three levels, the two upper tiers being suspended from roof trusses on steel rods and the lighting and sound systems encompass the whole of the Great Hall.

Manchester
STUDENTS UNION, UNIVERSITY OF MANCHESTER INSTITUTE OF SCIENCE AND TECHNOLOGY (UMIST), Altrincham Terrace, Manchester. *Cruickshank and Seward.* 1966.
≷ Manchester Piccadilly ☎ 061-236 9114
  One of a number of similar exercises by this practice, this scheme, like its fellows, is in carefully detailed white concrete and has survived the years with dignity. The building acts as a student club and 160-bed hall of residence and includes dining facilities. Land values dictated a dense development, so study-bedrooms are contained in a tower with lounges and other communal areas in the podium. Construction is of structural concrete with large precast panels forming the walls of the study-bedrooms.

Newcastle under Lyme
KEELE UNIVERSITY STUDENTS UNION, Newcastle under Lyme, Staffs. *Stillman and Eastwick-Field.* 1963.
🚌 A525 ≷ Stoke on Trent 🚌 208, 215, 217, 218 ☎ Registrar 0782 621111
  The design of this building, one of the first student unions to be built after the war, attempts a unity of expression and a robustness in keeping with the gusto of student life. The external buildings are white limestone concrete and blue Staffordshire bricks. The domed roof covers the large double-height, multi-purpose hall. Providing the social needs for a wholly residential campus, it is a clear and perhaps heroic statement in an indifferent building setting.

Runcorn
THE BROW HOUSING ESTATE, Halton Brow Road, Runcorn, Cheshire. *Runcorn Development Corporation.* 1969 and 1970.
Awards: MoHLG Housing Design Commendation 1969; Civic Trust Commendation 1971.
🚌 north of town centre ≷ Runcorn 🚌 T4 from station or town centre
  This scheme broke new ground in the multi-function use of space. The layout integrates the housing with the landscape to create privacy and a variety of semi-public areas. Narrow roads and subtle geometry help control traffic speed and the character of the access routes. It is a seminal scheme and remains one of the most successful housing estates in Britain, though is now almost lost in its mature planting.

168

169

170

171

Runcorn
SCHREIBER FACTORY, Astmoor Industrial Estate, Astmoor Road, Runcorn, Cheshire. *Runcorn Development Corporation and Brock Carmichael Associates.* 1974; 1979.
Awards: Structural Steel Design Award 1975; Eternit International Prize for Architecture 1976.
≈ Runcorn ⛟ T4 ☎ 09285 60188

A very elegant building, this single storey rectangular block is one of the early super-sheds. The innovative roof structure comprising triangular lattice girders gives a clear-span interior with services housed within the girders. Paired orange steel stanchions supporting alternative girders are expressed externally contrasting with the black steel cladding and dark tinted glass. Wood waste from the manufacturing process is used to make the factory largely self-sufficient in energy.

Warrington
ADVANCE INDUSTRIAL UNITS, Calver Road, Winwick Quay, Warrington, Lancs. *Nicholas Grimshaw and Partners.* 1979.
Award: RIBA Award 1980.
⛟ off A49 ≈ Warrington ☎ 0925 51144

Winwick Quay 4 is a 300 sq m building containing speculative industrial units. It was a prototype for factory design, exploring flexibility, complementary servicing arrangements and image. The rectangular plan minimises the floor-to-wall ratio, allowing a high proportion of the budget to be spent on the external wall – a high quality curtain wall with systemised interchangeable panels and doors. A forerunner of many of the 80s factory systems, the cladding is now looking rather shabby.

Warrington
GENESIS INDUSTRIAL COMPLEX, Birchwood Science Park, Warrington, Lancs. *Warrington and Runcorn Development Corporation.* 1982.
⛟ junction of M6 and M62 ⛟ 586 and 86 from Warrington town centre ≈ Birchwood ☎ 0925 51144

Aimed at small advanced technology businesses, Genesis comprises some 9,500 sq m of office, industrial and laboratory space on the edge of Britain's first science park. The plan and section share something of the tube aesthetic established by the Sainsbury Centre in Norwich. Familiar industrial materials are used in exciting ways. A second phase provides centralised support systems for the tenant community.

Warrington
OAKWOOD 52 HOUSING, Curlew Grove, Pipit Lane, Blackcap Walk, Oakwood, Birchwood, Lancs. *Warrington and Runcorn Development Corporation.* 1981.
Awards: DoE Good Design in Housing Medal 1980; RIBA Commendation 1982.
⛟ south east of junction of M6 (J21) and M62 (J11) ⛟ 9 from Warrington Town Centre ≈ Birchwood

One of several good housing schemes in the New Town, this scheme comprises 120 rented homes. It represents a fundamental re-evaluation of rented housing design after the large soulless estates of the 60s. The primarily semi-detached houses are grouped along a tree lined avenue, informal lanes or front on to the main pedestrian spine. A variety of layouts and house types gives an attractive non-repetitive quality.

172

173

174

175

Southern

Aylesbury

BLEDLOW VILLAGE HOUSING, Lyde End, Bledlow, Aylesbury, Bucks. *Aldington, Craig and Collinge.* 1977.

Awards: DoE Award for Good Design in Housing 1978; Civic Trust Award 1978; RIBA Commendation 1978; Brick Development Association Award 1979.

🚗 off B4009 Chinnor to Princes Risborough Road 🚆 Princes Risborough ☎ 0844 291228

This delightful group of six houses nestles comfortably into the old village setting. Designed as high quality rented homes for local people, the scheme has a distinct feeling of enclosure and homeliness. The houses are quite small, but an illusion of space is created by the use of two heights of monopitch roofs and full height glazing for the living-room walls. But it is really the quality of materials and detailing that sets this development apart.

Aylesbury

HADDENHAM VILLAGE HOUSING, Townside, Haddenham, Aylesbury, Bucks. *Aldington, Craig and Collinge.* 1968.

Award: RIBA Award 1970.

🚗 off A418 🚌 from Thame or Aylesbury 🚆 Thame or Aylesbury ☎ 0844 291228

This group of three houses owes much to 50s and 60s Scandinavian influences. Particularly characteristic is the white render finish to the walls, the tiled monopitch roof, the timber bar detailing over the windows and the integration of the group within the landscape.

Basingstoke

FORT HILL COMPREHENSIVE SCHOOL, Kenilworth Road, Basingstoke, Hants. *Hampshire County Council Architect's Department.* 1978.

Awards: Civic Trust 1980; RIBA Commendation 1982.

🚗 off A339 🚆 Basingstoke 🚌 320, 321 ☎ School Office 0256 54311

With its high, carefully composed roofs and pleasant landscaping, this school made a significant break from the post-war "box" tradition. Arranged around a series of planted courtyards and walkways, it is built of brick, timber and glass with deep overhanging eaves. Sadly, the interior with its gloomy deep plan spaces and suspended ceilings does not exhibit the same level of concern. Also of interest is the Four Lanes Primary School at nearby North Chineham, designed by the same architects.

176

177

178

Basingstoke
GATEWAY HOUSE OFFICES, Basing View, Basingstoke, Hants. *Arup Associates*. 1976.
Awards: Business and Industry Premier Award 1977; Civic Trust Commendation 1978; RIBA Award 1979; British Gas Energy Management Award 1980.
≠ Basingstoke ☎ 0256 20262

Externally, this building appears as a mechanical hill embodying a dialogue between technology and nature. The modular design steps back at each level to reveal a series of enchanting gardens in the air. It is an accomplished example of a design approach which integrates energy efficiency, humane working conditions and technology to produce an alternative to the usual office block.

Bracknell
BMW DISTRIBUTION CENTRE, Ellisfield Avenue, Bracknell, Berks. *Nicholas Grimshaw Partnership*. 1980.
A3095 from Bracknell ☎ 0344 26565

This is an elegant example of lightweight panel and glass construction. Appropriately sleek and well crafted, a long low office block fronts the warehouse, sharing the same white cladding. The showroom, offices and restaurant exhibit a consistent integration of construction, services and fittings. This is the architecture of efficiency – repetitive, cool and rather bland.

Bracknell
POINT ROYAL FLATS, Rectory Lane, Easthampstead, Bracknell, Berks. *Arup Associates*. 1964.
off A3095 ≠ Bracknell No access to interior

This is an example of the now dated architectural vision of towers set in a flowing landscape. The building is still elegant, the faceted block, poised above the ground on its central core with dished car park beneath. But unfortunately the in-situ concrete base has weathered badly, though the upper precast units have fared better.

Eastleigh
CRESTWOOD COMPREHENSIVE SCHOOL AND COMMUNITY CENTRE, Shakespeare Road, Boyatt Wood, Eastleigh. *Hampshire County Council Architect's Department*. 1981.
off Chandlers Ford by-pass ≠ Eastleigh 41, 44 ☎ 0703 641232

Architects have often sought to encourage interaction between school and the public. Here the idea has been implemented, resulting in an extraordinary broad, curved glazed "street". The school is arranged on either side with most of the classrooms facing away from the thoroughfare. Though cold and overdone, the "street" interior is worth seeing with its yellow staircases, trees and café tables. Glazed and with controlled ventilation, the street is an interesting exploration of the conservatory as providing additional economic space.

179

180

181

182

Eastleigh
ROOKWOOD INFANTS SCHOOL, Penhurst Way, Boyatt Wood, Eastleigh. *Hampshire County Council Architect's Department.* 1981.
⇌ Eastleigh ☎ 0703 618705
This bold, ingenious building has a triangular theme, picked up in the plan, landscaping and even the windows. Inside there is a delightful airy atmosphere due to the positioning of the glazing. External detailing, while direct, may be optimistic. The building makes an interesting contrast to the nearby Crestwood School (above).

Great Missenden
PUBLIC LIBRARY, High Street, Great Missenden, Bucks. *Buckinghamshire County Architect's Department.* 1970.
Award: Civic Trust Commendation 1971.
🚗 off A413 ⇌ Great Missenden
This split level two-storey structure takes advantage of the sloping riverside site in the central conservation area. The main lending library on the upper level has direct access from the high street, with administrative offices on the lower level bearing on to the car park. Load-bearing brickwork was chosen to retain the existing character of the street.

Havant
IBM MANUFACTURING PLANT, PO Box 6, Havant, Hants. *Arup Associates.* 1969-1981.
Awards: Structural Steel Award 1971; Financial Times Award 1972.
🚗 at junction of A27/B2149 ⇌ Havant ☎ 0705 486363
The original complex has been extended and altered without affecting its overall clarity. The early buildings present a low precast concrete façade with vision strip windows and are linked to an adjacent structure on a grassed podium. Described by one commentator as "a veritable temple to information processing", the later building is concrete clad and capped by a dark continuous glazed band hiding the offices. Typical of its era, the complex has successfully withstood the ravages of time.

Maidenhead
PUBLIC LIBRARY, St Ives Road, Maidenhead, Berks. *Ahrends Burton and Koralek.* 1973.
⇌ Maidenhead
This building has a commanding yet comfortable presence, uncompromisingly modern but fitting its context. Its design is indicative of the concern associated with this practice. A space deck hovers over a double-height volume with lending on the ground floor and reference and meeting rooms above. Red brick service areas are ingeniously inserted at angles creating a delightful atmosphere inside. Glazing runs around at space deck level and lower down is alternated with brick study bays. All works well except the reference section which is open to noise from other areas.

183

184

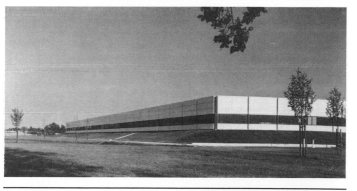

185

186

Milton Keynes
BRADWELL ABBEY INDUSTRIAL ESTATE, Milton Keynes, Bucks. *Milton Keynes Development Corporation Architects.* 1982.
🚗 A442 🚶 Milton Keynes 🚌 410, 441

In the wake of its large advance factory units of the mid 70s, MKDC moved down scale with these modest single storey AFUs for small and starter businesses. The units are of mirror glass and profiled steel sheeting in strong, fairly dark colours. The steel cladding curves around the eaves with curved glazing inserted at intervals to provide combined top and side lighting. Mirror glass curtain walling is used at the sides. This scheme shows how stylish industrial design can be, a point taken by the pension funds who funded this and other industrial schemes.

Milton Keynes
BRADWELL COMMON 1 HOUSING, Milton Keynes, Bucks. *Martin Richardson.* 1981. 🚗 junction of H5 and V7 🚶 Milton Keynes 🚌 440

Because of its central location at the junction of two principal roads and opposite the shopping centre, Bradwell 1 has a strong urban feel. The north, west and east façades are hard-edged terraces and the internal spaces comprise mews-like courts with under-house parking, and open squares. Colour is important in defining territory through brick banding and white render, and there is a clear attempt to link the various areas through a comprehensive footpath system.

Milton Keynes
CHAPTER HOUSE SINGLE PERSON HOUSING, Coffee Hall, Milton Keynes, Bucks. *MacCormac and Jamieson.* 1977.
Award: RIBA Commendation 1978.
🚶 Milton Keynes

Ninety single person flats have been squeezed into an inventive grid plan on a leftover triangular site. The scheme must rank as one of the highest quality of its type in Britain with its almost obsessive desire to create privacy and territorial control by residents from the entry car parking areas to the very private internal courtyards. Visitors are not welcome, but it is possible to pick out the distinctive roof form from vantage points around the perimeter.

Milton Keynes
EAGLESTONE HOUSING, Milton Keynes, Bucks. *Ralph Erskine.* 1979.
🚶 Milton Keynes

Designed by Erskine for housing packagers Bovis as a down market follow-up to Newcastle's Byker scheme, the estate comprises irregular terraces of fairly standard developer style houses. The special ingredients are arbitrary colour changes in brickwork, timber cladding and roof tiles, tacked on bow windows and rough timber porches. While Erskine's earlier schemes had unexpected colouring and patterning, here the rustic detailing looks as though it was all made in the same factory, with random selection of materials.

187

188

189

190

Milton Keynes
FISHERMEAD HOUSING, Milton Keynes, Bucks. *Milton Keynes Development Corporation Architects.* 1977.
≫ Milton Keynes ⟦⟧ 440, 441
 Part of the central area, Fishermead, like Conniborough and Springfield, is based on grid plans. The housing is arranged in great hollow squares, facing inward over back gardens to the squares and out to landscaped boulevards. On the street side, this has turned out to be the best preserved and pleasantest of all the early MKDC schemes. It is helped by the elaborate "boulevard" road system and carefully selected planting.

Milton Keynes
KILN FARM ADVANCE FACTORY UNITS, Kiln Farm, Milton Keynes, Bucks. *Milton Keynes Development Corporation Industry Group.* 1971–1973.
≫ Milton Keynes ⟦⟧ 410, 420
 These were early experiments in standardised factory design using flat roofs supported by slender columns and lattice girders through which services could be threaded. A specially-developed plastic-coated pressed metal panel gives the units the appearance of giant containers, with substitute window and ventilation panels inserted as required. But cost problems in maintaining the units and replacing the panels and the experimental nature of the scheme led the architects on to less visually adventurous industrial schemes until the late 70s.

Milton Keynes
MILTON KEYNES SHOPPING CITY, Central Milton Keynes, Bucks. *Milton Keynes Development Corporation Architects.* 1980.
Award: RIBA Award 1980.
≫ Milton Keynes
 A vast mirror glazed megastructure, the centre is surrounded by a formal array of malls and courtyards. Shopping is on the ground floor with service access at first floor level, so eliminating the visible presence of delivery trucks. Here the architects have straightened out the road patterns to align with the midwinter sun, the centre being set between Midwinter Boulevard and Silbury. Andrew Mahaddi's brilliantly inventive public pleasure facility, with glass bridge, tunnels and trick details culled from Italian Renaissance gardens, is intended as a miniature Silbury Hill. A prehistoric cosmic symbol is paved into one of the large courtyards.

Milton Keynes
NEATH HILL HOUSING, Neath Hill, Milton Keynes, Bucks. *Milton Keynes Development Corporation Architects.* 1980.
≫ Milton Keynes ⟦⟧ 410, 425, 426
 Designed at a time when public objections to Milton Keynes' "space age" image were rife, Neath Hill was the city's first serious attempt at Neovernacular styling. Its roads wiggle and there is a plethora of sub-Victorian and perhaps Edwardian brickwork detailing. The "olde worlde" village centre has acres of rather bright brick paving and a clock tower in busy timber scaffoldwork.

191

192

193

194

Milton Keynes
NETHERFIELD HOUSING, Milton Keynes, Bucks. *Milton Keynes Development Corporation Architects*. 1981.
≋ Milton Keynes 🚐 420

Conceived as a regular array of houses reading like a rectangular block with a regular grid subdivision extruded up from the ground, this scheme was influenced by theories of cosmic order – and probably the designs of the Italian group Superstudio. But despite attempts to regularise the sloping site, it was not in the end possible to achieve consistently level roofing. Of some interest is the small shopping centre, one side of which has an arcade supported by angled concrete slabs and originally designed to broadcast the name of the estate to passing motorists. A diagonal slash through the centre was intended to accommodate an old hedgerow on the alignment of a ley line. Sadly, most of it died during construction.

Milton Keynes
STACEY BUSHES INDUSTRIAL ESTATE, Stacey Bushes, Milton Keynes, Bucks. *Milton Keynes Development Corporation Architects*. 1979.
≋ Milton Keynes 🚐 441

Not far from Bradwell Abbey, the bright green factory units of Stacey Bushes present one of the few interesting set piece views of Milton Keynes from the train or motorway. Their distinctive deep profile corrugated asbestos cement walls and roofs are split down the middle by a triangular-section run of rooflights, continuing round the end eaves and down to the ground. The curved eaves disguise gutters behind.

Milton Keynes
WOUGHTON-ON-THE-GREEN HOUSING, Lucas Place, Woughton-on-the-Green, Milton Keynes, Bucks. *John Winter and Associates*. 1976.
Award: Brick Development Association Certificate of Merit 1981.
≋ Milton Keynes 🚐 495

Sited at the interface between the old village and the Milton Keynes linear park, this group of 51 houses was designed as a hard edge between the two. To give all the homes a parkland view, the section is stepped with two-storey units raised above single-storey old persons' flats. The expressed brick cross-walls and open frontages give simplicity while allowing privacy and identity to each house.

Minster Lovell
MINSTER LOVELL CONFERENCE CENTRE, Minster Lovell Mill, Minster Lovell, nr Oxford. *Edward Cullinan Architects*. 1969.
🚐 off A40 ☎ 0993 74441

An old mill, barn and malt house were converted into this residential conference centre. A long block of study-bedrooms set close to and overhanging the old garden wall makes a covered way linking the recreational facilities in the main house to the teaching rooms. Cotswold stone is used for walls and roofs with boldly sculptural oak joinery. Sitting comfortably in the landscape, this complex is a model of modern architecture reinterpreting vernacular forms and details in an appropriate way.

195

196

197

198

Oxford
BRASENOSE COLLEGE, STAIRCASES L16 AND L17, Oxford. *Powell & Moya*. 1961.
≈ Oxford
This small group of buildings is one of the finest in Oxford. The architects have inserted on a very small site some 30 study-bedrooms and ancillary spaces. At the broadest part of this long narrow site a four-storey block contains most of the rooms, while at ground level seven single storey rooms look into two small courtyards. The buildings are faced in Portland stone, and large sheer stone walls contrast with vertical bands of windows. These are carefully modulated with cross bands of rough concrete at slab and low sill levels.

Oxford
CUMBERBATCH QUAD, TRINITY COLLEGE, Oxford. *Robert Maguire and Keith Murray*. 1966.
≈ Oxford
This complex was cleverly conceived to give Trinity two new quads and to Blackwell's Bookshop, the Norrington Room, an enormous underground salesroom. A grey concrete block set on a recessed blue-black plinth houses the study-bedrooms, with projecting windows forming small bays beneath the overhanging slate roofs. The Cumberbatch building itself stands as an elegant pavilion terminating the larger quad. A panelled meeting room and lecture theatre are arranged on the lower level: above are fellows' and graduates' rooms set around a top-lit central spiral stair. In all, the complex is an excellent example of intensive and imaginative development in a tight urban space .

Oxford
FLOREY BUILDING, THE QUEEN'S COLLEGE, St Clements, Oxford. *James Stirling*. 1971.
≈ Oxford ☎ 0865 24811
Stirling's unmistakable language of red tiling, strong concrete structure and patent glazing is evident in this horseshoe-shaped residential block. A solid "blind" wall forms the public front, with a "soft" glazed inner wall facing on to a private communal space. The podium contains the dining-room and kitchen. Twin vertical circulation towers are linked by a glazed bridge to the main block. Sadly, this building may be as unsuccessful as a living space as it is brilliant in its formal inventiveness.

Oxford
GARDEN BUILDING, ST HILDA'S COLLEGE, Cowley Place, Oxford. *Alison and Peter Smithson*. 1970.
≈ Oxford
This interesting pavilion links two unrelated buildings at ground level, enclosing part of the college garden. Contemporary design preoccupations are present in the clear separation of the structure from the glazed walls and the chamfered corners. The plan too is clearly stated. But the simplicity belies the concern to humanise the concept diagram with particularly careful detailing throughout. Outside, the planted lattice screen has the greatest impact, creating a veil of privacy and making this a true garden pavilion.

199

200

201

202

Oxford

KEBLE COLLEGE EXTENSION, Blackhall and Museum Roads, Oxford. *Ahrends Burton and Koralek.* Phase I 1972; Phase II 1976.
Award: RIBA Award 1978.
≈ Oxford ☎ Bursar 0865 59201

Like Stirling's Florey Building, this is a built concept diagram keeping the town out and the college in, with no attempt to integrate with Butterfield's brickwork. A blank brick wall marks the sinuous boundary turning back to enclose a courtyard. Inside is all glass and though privacy is a problem, the whole suits the landscape. Outside the streetscape is successfully continued. The extension can best be seen as a successful state of the art, designed at a time when clarity of concept was considered all a building needed.

Oxford

LAW, ENGLISH AND STATISTICAL LIBRARIES, Manor Road, Oxford. *Sir Leslie Martin and Colin St John Wilson.* 1964.
Award: Civic Trust Award.
≈ Oxford

Three libraries form a single inter-related group, each independent but sharing some facilities. The central node for each component is the reading room, square in plan, galleried and top-lit. The three units are brought together around an external approach stair, while the reading rooms rising up above the surrounding levels identify each faculty building within the group.

Oxford

SAINSBURY BUILDING, WORCESTER COLLEGE, Worcester Place, Oxford. *MacCormac Jamieson and Pritchard.* 1982.
≈ Oxford ☎ Bursar 0865 247251

This residential complex is evidently of a different architecture than many in Oxford. With few heroic pretensions, it aims to be a small scale mini-village. But there are touches of formal gesturing in the rear gatehouse with its notional split pediment and the formal symmetry of the plan along the diagonal axis. As a living space it could hardly be more attractive, but the detailing hints at over-design with too many architectural tricks in a confined space and a hectic use of every available material.

Oxford

ST ANTHONY'S COLLEGE DINING HALL AND COMMON ROOM, Oxford. *Howell, Killick, Partridge and Amis.* 1970.
Awards: RIBA Award 1971; Concrete Society Award 1971.
≈ Oxford ☎ Domestic Bursar 0865 59651

Possibly the best example of this practice's style, this three-storey central pavilion stands in a large walled garden. The upper floors are set over a deeply recessed colonnaded walled ground floor with octagonal frame columns on a brick plinth rising out of the lawn. Above, precast concrete cladding panels are varied to read as separate elements. Inside, exposed concrete and brick make spare rugged spaces with the coffered ceiling exposed on the upper floors. At nearby St Anne's College the Wolfson and Payne Buildings are in a similar strongly sculptural language.

203

204

205

206

Oxford
SIR THOMAS WHITE BUILDING, ST JOHN'S COLLEGE, Oxford. *Arup Associates*. 1976.
Awards; Concrete Society Award 1976; RIBA Award 1981.
≈ Oxford ☏ Domestic Bursar 0865 47671

This large L-shaped residential complex forms a new quadrangle with the adjacent buildings. Two formal ideas are successfully combined; following the traditional arrangement of horizontal buildings, the blocks are linked at ground level to the college circulation, while the blocks themselves are a series of isolated, but linked vertically, proportioned pavilions of differing heights. The result is a rich variety of scales from the large scale of the quad to the smaller scales of the individual pavilions, each with meticulously detailed elements of glass, stone and concrete.

Oxford
WOLFSON COLLEGE, Linton Road, Oxford. *Powell and Moya*. 1974.
Awards: RIBA Award 1975; Concrete Society Award 1975.
≈ Oxford

This new post-graduate college complex has all the components of a traditional college, plus family accommodation. Apart from the ungainly pyramidal roof of the dining hall, the various elements are suppressed within an overall discipline. The exposed aggregate concrete frame makes a strong formal pattern against the dark glass infill walls and white-painted blockwork. This building is perhaps less successful than Powell and Moya's earlier work at Blue Boar Quad, and at Corpus Christi and Brasenose Colleges where there is a greater richness of form and texture.

Portsmouth
CENTRAL LIBRARY, Guildhall Square, Portsmouth, Hants. *Portsmouth City Architect's Department*. 1976.
≈ Portsmouth ☏ 0705 819311

Set at the south corner of the Guildhall Square, the Public Library is a far more assured piece of work than the adjacent Civic Offices (below). Large cantilevers are used to achieve deep horizontal bands of buff mosaic and narrow deep-set continuous glazing. These forms contrast with the in-situ concrete vertical tubes which house the escape stairs. Inside, pleasant, large open plan areas are punctured vertically by an open stairwell. In all the building is comfortable and popular and has weathered well.

Portsmouth
CIVIC OFFICES, Guildhall Square, Portsmouth, Hants. *Teggin and Taylor*. 1976.
Award: RIBA Commendation 1977.
≈ Portsmouth ☏ 0705 822251

The focus of the Esher plan to rebuild war-damaged Portsmouth, the offices and library define a large brick-paved square around the historic Guildhall. Shops and cafés originally planned for the space were axed, making it a bleak area fortunately enlivened by reflections of the Guildhall in the glass walled Civic Offices, which wrap around the north and east sides of the square. Though visually striking, the six-storey building has suffered considerable solar gain and heat loss problems.

207

208

209

210

Portsmouth

FREWEN LIBRARY, PORTSMOUTH POLYTECHNIC, Cambridge Road, Portsmouth, Hants. *Ahrends Burton and Koralek*. 1977.

just south of Guildhall ⇌ Portsmouth ☎ Deputy Librarian 0705 827681

The vertically glazed stepped roof makes a powerful impact, especially at night. As only half of the library is complete, strange slices of the building are exposed to view. Reinforced in-situ concrete, concrete block and glazing are used in a way characteristic of this practice. Inside are three levels, the first and second set back like trays supported by elegant yellow roof trusses. Controlled natural light is admitted through the rooflights into the deep plan. The complex roof has created problems, but when complete this accomplished building will provide a stylish core to the Polytechnic.

Portsmouth

IBM HEAD OFFICE, North Harbour, Cosham, Portsmouth, Hants. *Arup Associates*. 1976-82.

Award: Phase III: Financial Times Industrial Architecture Commendation 1978.

off M27/A27 ⇌ Portsmouth ☎ 0705 321212

The first phase of this complex is a straightforward and undistinguished series of modular office elements. But the most recent phase is more interesting, comprising three office pods whose stepped façades provide roof terraces. A full height barrel-vaulted glazed street links the three and is entered beneath a cascade of glazing housing escalators and reception. The bravado of the design obscures awkward junctions and very long walking distances in a building that is virtually a small town.

Portsmouth

IBM MARKETING ADMINISTRATION OFFICES, 1 Northern Road, Cosham, Portsmouth, Hants. *Foster Associates*. 1971.

Award: RIBA Award 1972; Structural Steel Design Award 1972.

M27 ⇌ Cosham or Havant ☎ 0705 370911

Now rather bland with its bronzed glass skin, this building created great interest on completion. Designed as a temporary building, it drew together the ideas of the systems approach in a pure, more integrated way than had previously been known in Britain. All the elements are there – clear-span lightweight steel structure, modular sealed lightweight skin, integrated servicing and controlled environment. Inside the building shows signs of wear and tear, but the exterior is still pristine and unobtrusive.

Reading

FOBNEY WATER TREATMENT WORKS, Rose Kiln Lane, Reading. *Terry Farrell Partnership*. 1982.

A33 ⇌ Reading 3, 4, 5, 6, 7, 8, 15 ☎ 0734 55822

Sitting atop a purification tank, this H-plan building has reflective glass cladding and a glazed barrel vault extending its full length covers the main corridor. The central foyer features a cascade of glazing, the curves of which are intended to relate to the water. The high tech, clip-together construction has witty touches such as overscaled steps and lighting columns framing the observation areas. It is a confident and stylish example of the design potential of a basically utilitarian structure.

211

212

213

214

Waterlooville

WATERLOOVILLE BAPTIST CHURCH, 368 London Road, Waterlooville, Hants. *Michael Manser Associates.* 1967.

A3 ☎ 07014 51169/59167

Very much of its time, this striking church employs exposed steel, glass and brick in a direct, well-proportioned manner. The almost square interior is flooded with light from glazed side walls and a rooflight over the altar. The scheme includes a badminton hall, crèche and meeting rooms. Maintenance is clearly a problem and the building is now subsiding into shabbiness in keeping with its surroundings.

Wokingham

ST CRISPIN'S COMPREHENSIVE SCHOOL, Bracknell Road, Wokingham, Berks. *Ministry of Education (now DES) Development Group.* 1953.

A329 ☎ School Office 0734 781144

The first of the Ministry's attempts to test new teaching ideas and economic labour saving construction methods, this school has a light steel frame and dry-assembled modular components. Extensions have been added and the building has suffered like many of its contemporaries from roof and heating problems and poor insulation. But it has withstood heavy use and retains a light, airy quality, though is rather humourless and drips with social purpose.

Yately

NEWLANDS PRIMARY SCHOOL, Dungells Lane, Yately, Hants. *Hampshire County Council Architect's Department.* 1979.

Awards: Civic Trust Award 1982; Education School Building Design Award. 1982.

off A30 ☎ 0252 871188

Two high parallel pitched roofs are linked by a glazed and paved conservatory. This building is extremely well considered and significant for the way it fuses user requirements and environmental control. Inside there is a lovely sense of scale provided by the continuous door-height service duct, low partitions and glazing. The conservatory provides 20 per cent extra teaching space, while manually operated ridge vents allow natural ventilation.

215

216

217

South East

Ashford
MAGISTRATES' COURT, Tufton Street, Ashford, Kent. *Kent County Architect's Department.* 1978.

⇌ Ashford ☎ Clerk to the Magistrates 0233 23186

Torn apart by post-war planning, Ashford is dominated by a huge glazed office building, largely unlet and making a poor gesture to modern architecture. Rather than follow this self-conscious lead, the designers of the Magistrates' Court have opted for a low-key solution for this large building physically restrained by its small site. The task was not easy but they have coped admirably.

Bexhill
THORWOOD OLD PERSONS' HOME AND SHELTERED HOUSING, Turkey Road, Bexhill, East Sussex. *East Sussex County Architect's Department.* 1982.

🚌 off A2036 ⇌ Bexhill ☎ 0424 223442

Similar in style to the old persons' complex at Polehill near Eastbourne, this building manages to avoid an institutional atmosphere. Deep overhangs provide shade and give sheltered external walks, while most of the bedsits have angled glazing to admit afternoon sunlight. A central day centre provides a link with the outside world being visible to passers-by at ground and first floor levels. It is a very successful scheme offering residents a real sense of living in a comfortable community.

Brighton
GARDNER ARTS CENTRE, University of Sussex, Falmer, Brighton. *Sir Basil Spence, Bonnington and Collins.* 1971.

🚌 Brighton to Lewes Road 🚌 from Brighton to Falmer ⇌ Falmer ☎ Information Officer 0273 606755

Serving the entire region, the University arts complex houses theatre and exhibitions alongside the experimental arts. A restricted budget forced the design policy of creating as large a shell as possible leaving space allocation and fitting out to be completed as funds became available. The experimental theatre with its removable seating for up to 500 and three stages allows a variety of performance layouts. The foyer leads from the theatre into an art gallery and there are artists' studios and music practice rooms within the brick drums off the main theatre block.

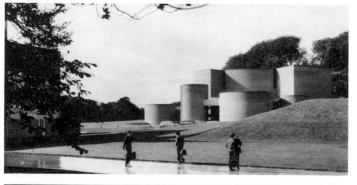

218

219

220

Bromley
SOUTH HILL COURT HOUSING, 107 Westmoreland Road, Bromley, Kent.
Edward Cullinan Architects. 1979.
≥ Bromley South ⚍ 126 ☎ Solon Housing Association 01-274 9990

A single building containing six four-bedroomed, eight three bed-roomed, ten two bedroomed and 12 single bedroomed apartments presents an urban façade to this former Edwardian avenue. The north facing street frontage retains an ordinary house-like character, while to the south terraces and balconies overlook a large shared garden. Stained timber balustrades, eaves and external stairs give an ornamental feel to the honey-coloured render and the specially fabricated plywood gates add a delightful touch.

Canterbury
LUXMORE HOUSE, THE KING'S SCHOOL, The Precincts, Canterbury, Kent. *Maguire and Murray.* 1981.
≥ Canterbury ☎ 0227 62963

Tucked into a pocket-handkerchief of a site alongside the Cathedral Choir School is Luxmore House, accommodating 55 boys, five day-girls, the housemaster and housekeeper. The ancient walls have been incorporated into the scheme which features steep tiled pitched roofs and walls with alternate courses of brick and blockwork. Wide overhanging eaves shade the windows below.

Canterbury
THE TREE HOUSE, 50 Hollow Lane, Canterbury, Kent. *Steve Skinner.* 1982.
⚍ A28 Ashford Road left off Wincheap Roundabout ≥ Canterbury ☎ Steve Skinner 0227 56167

Skinner's house, like many of his local schemes, incorporates passive solar principles. The L-shaped building features a central conservatory separated from the main house by a buffer-zone corridor which is entered through glazed doors. The living area can be opened out to include this space or partitioned off. Insulation levels are three times the statutory requirements and there are the usual small windows on the north façade with overhangs and pergolas on the south wall to limit heat gain. A severe winter has shown that the design works well with fuel bills approximately half those of a comparable conventional home.

Chatham
LLOYD'S ADMINISTRATIVE HEADQUARTERS, Gun Wharf, Chatham, Kent. *Arup Associates.* 1978.
Awards: Civic Trust Award 1980; Business and Industry Award 1980; RIBA Award 1981.
≥ Chatham ☎ Chief Executive 0634 407333

Best viewed from the train across the Medway, this building is identified by its pitched roofs, sweeping down the contours of the site and forming deep overhangs to the broad bands of windows. Like many Arup schemes, it is built on a square bay module to allow for internal flexibility. Arranged around two courtyards, the four office floors are planned to allow changes in size and location of the various departments. Working areas offer a comfortable environment and good outlook. This is a huge building which fits its site as though it had always been there.

221

222

223

224

Chatham
MEDWAY MAGISTRATES' COURT, The Brook, Chatham, Kent. *Howell, Killick, Partridge and Amis*. 1980.
≼ Chatham ☎ Clerk of the Court 0634 400341

Occupying a sloping site surrounded by mediocre post-war buildings, this court is an object lesson in restrained, carefully considered design. The appropriate environment and imagery is sustained by the overall control of architecture and detail. A remarkable sense of quality is achieved, despite often irreconcilable briefing constraints, though the calm of the courtrooms contrasts rather violently with the stark abruptness of the Kafka-esque "fine" counters.

Chichester
CHICHESTER FESTIVAL THEATRE, Chichester, West Sussex. *Powell Moya and Partners*. 1961.
≼ Chichester ☎ 0243 84437

Once fiercely controversial because of its innovative open stage layout, Chichester is now an established part of theatrical folklore. Built at a cost of £95,064, it provoked the *Architect's Journal* to comment on completion: "The virtues of this theatre are clear for all to see. It is an astonishing achievement for the cost and it is certainly one of the most exciting and unusual buildings to be put up for a long time."

Chichester
CHICHESTER THEOLOGICAL COLLEGE, Chichester, Sussex. *Ahrends Burton and Koralek*. 1965.
≼ Chichester ☎ Bursar 0243 783369

Set in a mature country garden, the new residential block forms a link between the existing college and chapel. The design was conceived as a series of walls of larger units enclosing smaller elements. Built of rugged materials, the building looks from the outside as if it were carved from one mass: inside the painted blockwork walls are enhanced by the interplay of light from sloping toplights and windows. While integrating well with the old college, the building stands in its own right as a fine piece of architecture.

Churt
EDDYSTONE COURT SHELTERED HOUSING, Churt, Surrey. *David Lea*. 1981.
🚌 Haslemere Road from Farnham ≼ Farnham 🚌 from Farnham to Churt ☎ Warden 0428 714173

Surprisingly, this scheme caused trauma among the local planners unlike the indifferent spec-built luxury homes that are its neighbours. Delays added 14 months to the contract and a 13.5 per cent increase in costs to the client. The buildings, with their simple frame construction, are truly beautiful. They conjure up the delight of traditional Japanese housing and the expertise of Frank Lloyd Wright.

225

226

227

228

Egham

CHEMISTRY BUILDING, ROYAL HOLLOWAY COLLEGE, University of London, Egham, Surrey. *Colquhoun and Miller.* 1968/69.

🚆 A4 ⇌ Egham ☏ 01-873 5351

This building takes advantage of a sloping site, stepping down west to east in an interlocking section. Stairs follow the slope connecting the different levels and a pedestrian mall running north to south links the common room, library and lecture theatres. By developing a design rationale of a long but small scale design, servicing and construction, the architects have given the building a high degree of adaptability and growth potential. It is a brilliant scheme, in the highest tradition of post-war educational buildings.

Gatwick

GATWICK AIRPORT, Gatwick, West Sussex. *YRM Architects and Planners.* In progress.

🚆 A23 or M23 from London ⇌ Gatwick ☏ Public Relations Manager 0293 503096

First mooted in 1955, Gatwick was the first airport to integrate road, rail and air transport and the first in Europe to adopt a pier access system. The original master-plan has responded well to expansion and changes in aircraft technology with the new circular northern satellite marking the culmination of the development. This is linked to the main terminal by an elevated rapid transit system. A second terminal, now on site, will eventually be connected to the main building and the railway station by the same means.

Gillingham

GILLINGHAM BUSINESS PARK, PHASE 2, Grant Close and Sherman Close, Gillingham, Kent. *Nicholas Grimshaw and Partners.* 1980.
Award: Architectural Design Project Award 1981.

🚆 A278 🚌 from Gillingham or Rainham ⇌ Gillingham or Rainham ☏ Estate Manager 0634 363997

One of four phases, this building is the archetypical highly serviced flexible shed. An external perimeter service system makes internal planning easy while the panel wall system can be adjusted to suit individual tenants' needs. The only fixed elements are the ground slab, steel frame and service ducting. The other phases are now complete and have picked up a string of awards, indicating their merit as high quality commercial buildings set on well-landscaped sites.

Gravesend

NATIONAL SEA TRAINING COLLEGE, Denton, Gravesend, Kent. *Lyons Israel Ellis.* 1967.

⇌ Gravesend ☏ Reception Officer 0474 63656

Designed to house some 600 naval trainees during a three-month course, this complex forms a quad with L-shaped dormitory block, classroom block and assembly hall and catering areas. Built before the Thames Barrier, the buildings were liable to flooding from the river and so are planned with a raised ground floor. It is a tough, ordered scheme which has stood up well to the hard knocks dealt by its temporary residents.

229

230

231

232

Guildford
GUILDFORD COURT STUDENT HOUSING, University of Surrey, Guildford. *Maguire and Murray.* 1970.
≈ Guildford ☎ 0483 576874
Surrey University's small student "town", down the hill from Edward Maufe's Guildford Cathedral, comprises 10 concrete block houses designed to a domestic scale. While halls of residence are generally disliked by students this finely detailed complex has achieved a quiet popularity.

Haslemere
OLIVETTI TRAINING CENTRE, Branksome Hilders, Hindhead Road, Haslemere, Surrey. *Edward Cullinan Architects.* 1972.
≈ Haslemere 🚌 219 ☎ Manager 0428 4011
An Edwardian country house provides the residential part of the training complex, the main functional building (below) having been added by James Stirling. Cullinan's conversion uses two notions developed in his earlier housing schemes: parallel circulation and servicing strips; and a hard façade balanced by a glazed counterpart. The result gives a diffuse and rambling plan a new clarity. This bold rationalisation is remarkably successful and stands well against Stirling's high-tech training school.

Haslemere
OLIVETTI TRAINING SCHOOL, Branksome Hilders, Hindhead Road, Haslemere, Surrey. *James Stirling and Partner.* 1972.
≈ Haslemere 🚌 219 ☎ Manager 0428 4011
Since this early high-tech scheme, Stirling has moved into a more eclectic Classical phase. This building along with the Runcorn housing marks the end of his adventure in Modern architecture. Constructed of prefabricated parts, two wings are connected by a glazed gallery which adjoins the main building. The classroom wings are of glass reinforced polyester panels clipped together and allowing for future extension. The glazed link block is approached by ramps and features motorised roll-around walls which can be opened to connect the cruciform multi-purpose space into the circulation area.

Hastings
HALTON FIRE STATION, The Ridge, Hastings, East Sussex. *East Sussex County Architect's Department.* 1977.
🚌 B2093 ≈ Hastings 🚌 421 ☎ 0424 422230
Fire stations are notoriously difficult to design and, apart from the London County Council's Edwardian efforts by Charles Canning Winmill, are often dismal structures. At Halton the conflicts are apparently reconciled, mainly by the use of a zinc-clad saw-tooth roof which links the disparate elements. The roof and its horizontal fascia form the most dominant feature, fitting snugly over the warm-coloured brick walls.

233

234

235

236

Horsham

CHRIST'S HOSPITAL ARTS CENTRE, Horsham, West Sussex. *Howell, Killick, Partridge and Amis*. 1975.

Award: RIBA Award 1975.

🚗 off A24 🚆 Christ's Hospital ☎ 0403 52709

Forming three sides of a courtyard, this extension includes classrooms, library and seminar room and a theatre for around 500. The existing music school has also been expanded to increase teaching accommodation. Red bricks create the new exterior, while inside the brickwork is painted white to set off the natural wood and red-stained timber finishes.

Leatherhead

THORNCROFT MANOR, Dorking Road, Leatherhead, Surrey. *Michael Manser Associates*. 1975.

Awards: Structural Steel Design Commendation 1976; RIBA Commendation 1977.

🚗 off A24 🚆 Leatherhead ☎ 0372 376756

The objective here was to create a new building which still allowed Sir Robert Taylor's 18th-century manor house to dominate. The height of the extension is therefore governed by the eaves of the existing house and the proportions have been determined by the Golden Section in plan and elevation. The mirror glazed result is an unusual building, highly courageous in its approach.

Leatherhead

THORNDIKE THEATRE, Church Street, Leatherhead, Surrey. *Roderick Ham and Partners*. 1969.

Awards: RIBA Award 1970; Building for the Disabled Award 1970.

🚆 Leatherhead ☎ 0372 376211/377677

Designed for a repertory company, this fine theatre has a single tier auditorium with 526 seats in wide-spaced rows. Access to the foyers is through a four-storey shop and office block on Church Street. The foyers sweep around the auditorium on three levels giving access from the rear. Facilities for the disabled include a special lift and space for wheelchairs in the auditorium.

Maidstone

MAIDSTONE DISTRICT GENERAL HOSPITAL PHASE 1, Hermitage Lane, Barming, Maidstone, Kent. *Powell Moya and Partners*. 1983.

🚗 off A20 🚆 Barming, Maidstone East or Maidstone West 🚌 Hospital special from Barming ☎ 0622 29000

Here the architects have succeeded in overcoming the enormous problems of hospital planning to produce architecture. The first phase comprises 300 beds with the usual medical and administrative facilities, the main clinical element being planned in line with DHSS "Nucleus" principles. A second phase will add 112 beds. The main design component of the scheme is the cruciform "template", used to form interconnecting two-storey blocks. This device breaks down the mass, while external courtyards and gardens give a domestic scale to this very large complex.

237

239

238

240

Poole

HOUSE, 12A Western Avenue, Branksome Park, Poole, Dorset. *Richard Horden.* 1974.

Awards: RIBA Commendation 1978.

≥ Bournemouth ☏ Richard Horden 01-435 3430/01-637 5431

   This single storey house occupies a site in a lush wooded suburb of Poole. A simple exposed steel frame with floor-to-ceiling glazing set beneath a roof with overhangs on the east and west façades produce a delightfully crisp modern building – a stark, but breathtaking contrast to the Noddyland vernacular that encroaches on all flanks.

Tadworth

UOP FRAGRANCES HEADQUARTERS AND MANUFACTURING PLANT, Pitwood Park, Waterfield, Tadworth, Surrey. *Richard Rogers and Partners.* 1974.

Awards: RIBA Commendation 1975; Structural Steel Design Award 1975.

🚗 A25 to Banstead then Tadworth ≥ Tadworth

   One of a series of "zip-up" schemes by Rogers, this building is completely prefabricated above slab level. A wide span lattice steel structure is clad with heavily insulated composite panels. The panels of glass reinforced concrete on an expanded polystyrene core incorporate large windows, vent unit and an ingenious "up and over" loading bay door. The building is finished with lime green epoxy coating and glazing joints and panels are sealed by black compression gaskets.

Tunbridge Wells

ST AUGUSTINE'S ROMAN CATHOLIC CHURCH AND PRIESTS' HOUSE, Crescent Road, Tunbridge Wells, Kent. *Maguire and Murray.* 1975.

≥ Tunbridge Wells ☏ 0892 22525

   Externally unprepossessing with its vertically-hung tiles, brickwork and pitched roof, inside this church is magnificent. This may be due to "fearsome" planning constraints in an area dominated by the work of Decimus Burton. Set on a sloping site in the Calverly Park Conservation Area, the building includes the worship area at first floor level with accommodation for four priests and a housekeeper beneath. An intricate timber roof supported on four pillars with beam links appears to float above the walls and internal detailing is kept simple creating a feeling of calm and tranquillity.

241

242

243

South West

Bath
HERMAN MILLER FACTORY, Locksbrook Road, Bath. *Farrell/Grimshaw Partnership*. 1977.
Awards: Financial Times Industrial Architecture Award 1977; Structural Steel Design Award 1977; Business and Industry Certificate of Merit 1977; RIBA Award 1978; Civic Trust Commendation 1978.
🚉 Bath 🚌 A4 Lower Bristol Road (½ mile from Bath) 🚗 4 ☎ 0225 28477
   This factory on the banks of the Avon is the jewel of an otherwise sleazy part of Bath. It put Farrell/Grimshaw on the architectural map and led to numerous imitations by other architects. Designed around a steel frame, the grp sandwich wall panels are easily removed to give flexibility in the positioning of doors, windows, louvres and service outlets.

Bath
ROTORK CONTROLS FACTORY, Brassmill Lane Trading Estate, Bath. *Farrell/Grimshaw Partnership*. 1972.
🚌 off Upper Bristol Road from Bath 🚉 Bath 🚗 4, 339 ☎ 0225 28451
   Flexibility is the essence of this scheme. Four weeks before completion the clients changed their production methods, but the building was able to accommodate the new system. An identical building has now been constructed for Rotork in the USA. Despite 10 years' heavy use, the Bath building still looks smart and attractive.

Bath
ROTORK CONTROLS FACTORY, Brassmill Lane Trading Estate, Bath. *Leonard Manasseh Partnership*. 1966.
Award: Financial Times Industrial Architecture Commendation 1966.
🚌 off Upper Bristol Road from Bath 🚉 Bath 🚗 4, 339 ☎ 0225 28451
   Elegant and crisp when completed this factory is now beginning to show its age and could do with a thorough clean. The building looks its best at night when the glazing and fine latticed steel structure is illuminated from within.

244

245

246

Bristol
CATHEDRAL CHURCH OF SS PETER AND PAUL, Clifton Park, Clifton, Bristol. *Percy Thomas Partnership.* 1973.
Awards: RIBA Bronze Medal and Award 1974; Concrete Society Award 1974.
≱ Bristol 🚍 7, 8, 22 ☎ Administrator 0272 738 411
This is a work of considerable importance, reaching a degree of competence and high quality craftsmanship all too rarely found in contemporary church architecture. Though the interior quality is not matched on the outside, the building seeming to turn its back to the main approach, and the fleche motif appearing applied rather than growing out of the structure, this is the best of a series of post-war cathedrals.

Bristol
CEGB SOUTH WEST REGION HEADQUARTERS, Bedminster Down, Bristol. *Arup Associates.* 1978.
Awards: Business and Industry Award 1979; RIBA Award 1980; Civic Trust Award 1980; Financial Times Commendation 1980.
🚗 off A35 from Bristol to Taunton ≱ Bristol 🚍 28 ☎ 0272 648111
This fine office complex sits atop the Down, enjoying superb views towards Clifton Gorge and the coast. The 24,000 sq m accommodation is arranged in four pavilions around a central hall. A central "street" from the main reception links the open plan pavilions to laboratories and social facilities. Energy conservation is a key feature, maximum use being made of natural energy sources and internal waste heat. All materials have been carefully specified and the detailing is flawless.

Bristol
HOUSING, High Kingsdown, St Michael's Hill, Bristol. *Whicheloe Macfarlane Partnership in association with the JT Group of Companies.* 1974.
Awards: DoE Good Design in Housing Gold Medal 1974; Belgian National Housing Institute 1974; RIBA Award 1975.
🚗 behind Bristol Royal Infirmary ≱ Bristol 🚍 13 ☎ 0272 299861
Occupying a derelict bomb site, this scheme comprises 103 privately developed houses and flats. The two-storey houses form the heart, arranged in a tight L-shaped zig-zag terraces between a system of footways. High walls provide privacy and delightful sheltered gardens. Garages are grouped around the perimeter allowing no through traffic. The scheme has survived the rigours of weather and vandalism relatively intact.

Bristol
SHORLAND HOUSE, Beaufort Road, Bristol. *Bob Organ and Jeremy Gould.* 1975.
🚗 A4176 from Bristol ≱ Bristol 🚍 47
This sheltered housing on the outskirts of Bristol is a crisp and tidy scheme that set the scene for many followers. The neat detailing on the concrete columns and slabs looked exceptionally smart when the building was young and fitted well with the rectangular lines of the structure. Weathering has mellowed the effect, but the building is still strikingly powerful.

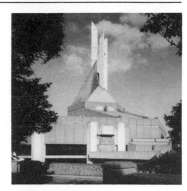

247

248

249

250

Bristol
W D AND H O WILLS FACTORY AND OFFICES, Hartcliffe, Nr Bristol. *YRM with Skidmore Owings and Merrill.* 1974.
Awards: RIBA Award 1976; British Steel Corporation, Premier Design Award 1976; Financial Times Industrial Architecture Commendation 1976.
🚗 off M4 ⇌ Bristol 🚌 10, 27, 36, 46, 74, 77, 78 ☎ 0272 641111

External walls of the factory are of bronzed glazing in stove-painted aluminium frames and earth-coloured ribbed metal sheet. The fascia, exposed stanchions and roof trusses are of Cor-Ten weathering steel, thought to be appropriate for the landscaped parkland setting. This same high standard is echoed in the offices. This building, bridging an artificial lake, has a two-storey L-shaped podium clad with precast panels and five-storey glazed tower with exposed Cor-Ten frame. The steel has weathered well, though the ghastly barbed wire perimeter fence adds nothing.

Bude
HOUSE, Pathfields, Stratton, Bude, Cornwall. *The Jonathan Ball Practice.* 1980.
Awards: Cornish Buildings Group Annual Award 1982. RIBA Award 1983.
🚗 off A39

This stylish timber-framed house occupies a backland site overlooking the dramatic north Cornwall coastline. Built by its owner, it is finished externally with deep blue diagonal timber boarding, the eaves, door and window frames picked out in bright red. Inside, the double-height central hall is approached on the diagonal to give space and depth to an essentially simple plan.

Chippenham
HERMAN MILLER WAREHOUSE, Bath Road, Chippenham, Wilts. *Nicholas Grimshaw and Partners.* 1983.
🚗 junction of A4 and A355 ⇌ Chippenham 🚌 231, 232 ☎ 0249 657011

Standing at a prominent road junction on the outskirts of Chippenham the warehouse is in full view of the main London to Bristol railway line. A simple internal steel structure supports an array of clip-on interchangeable super-plastic aluminium panels coated in three shades of bright blue. A superb office suite set between the sweeping entrance porches is used as a showcase for Herman Miller's latest office furniture. Future plans include trebling the size of the extendable building.

Exeter
EXETER UNIVERSITY LIBRARY, University Campus, St David's, Exeter. *John Crowther and Associates.* 1983.
⇌ Exeter

Exeter has enjoyed a significant post-war building programme. Close to the centre is the University campus sporting a number of distinguished buildings. The most recent addition is the library. Set to the south of the realigned Stocker Road on the same axis as the Great Hall, this building features multi-coloured brick facing, harmonising with other schemes in the complex. Windows are kept to a minimum, and are set in small slatted bronze frames.

251

252

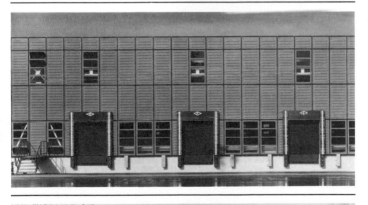

253

254

Exeter
LONDON AND MANCHESTER ASSURANCE COMPANY HEADQUAR-
TERS, Winslade Manor, Clyst St Mary, Exeter. *Powell, Moya and Partners.*
1978.
Awards: RIBA Award 1979; Civic Trust Awards 1980.
🚌 A377 🚉 Exeter 🚌 339, 371
   Set in fine parkland, Winslade Manor comprises an 18th-century manor
house and stables. The architects have added a modern building to accom-
modate 500 staff. Features include white bush-hammered concrete col-
umns and expressed floor slab edges with grey Cornish granite aggregate.
The new block responds to and respects the overall scale of the old house
without spoiling the views across the landscape.

Exeter
SHILHAY HOUSING, Commercial Road, Exeter. *MWT Architects.* 1978.
Awards: DoE Housing Award 1979. Arnold Sayers Award 1979.
🚉 Exeter
   This significant and eye-catching development sits on the banks of the
River Exe. The layout is of high standard with dwelling plans situated to
give good views from windows and balconies. The grouping of houses
around landscaped courts gives a pleasant sense of space and enclosure,
and a feeling of community pervades the whole development.

Flax Bourton
ONE-OFF HOUSES, Post Office Lane, Flax Bourton. *Bob Organ and Tom
Organ.* 1973.
🚌 A370 from Bristol
   These fine modern houses are tucked away at the end of a sleepy village
lane and are unusual for such a conservation-conscious area. An
excellent, co-ordinated set of five dwellings, this development illustrates
perfectly that modern architecture can have a place in a rural setting.

Plymouth
PLYMOUTH MAGISTRATES' COURT, St Andrew's Street, Plymouth.
Devon County Council Architect's Department. 1980.
Awards: RIBA Award 1980.
🚉 Plymouth
   This building brings new life to a hitherto depressed part of the city centre. Responding to the challenges set by neighbouring buildings, it reflects
their materials but is unashamedly modern. Particular skill is shown in
relating the scheme to the adjacent parish church, the 15th-century Prys-
ten House and recently restored Elizabethan Merchant's House. Cornish
granite sets, salvaged from the site and from redundant city roads, have
been laid around the new building, undoubtedly helping to retain and enhance the original character of this historic area.

255

256

257

258

Shipton-under-Wychwood
HOUSE, Shipton-under-Wychwood. *Stout and Litchfield.* 1964.

The planners were startled by the architects' designs for this unconventional weekend Cotswold cottage and permission was only granted after a hard fought public enquiry. The house comprises a long kitchen diner with lounge at one end and a cluster of three bedrooms at the other. A small lake winds its way around three sides of the house, providing a delightful though rather damp setting.

Swindon
BRUNEL SHOPPING CENTRE, Swindon. *Douglas Stephen and Partners with BDP.* 1975.
Award: RIBA Award 1977.
≋ Swindon

This is one of the best shopping centres in the UK. The designers were clearly influenced by the great railway engineer after whom the complex is named and his magnificent arched station roofs. Their application of his approach to this scheme works perfectly, particularly as Swindon has always been a railway town. Though the form suggests Victorian engineering, the use of modern lightweight materials and techniques is very much of the present day. The complex has weathered well and is a resounding success, giving Swindon a distinctive skyline feature.

Swindon
OASIS LEISURE CENTRE, North Star Avenue, Swindon. *The Gillinson Partnership (formerly Gillinson Barnett and Partners).* 1976.
Awards: Gold Medal, Design Awards Competition of American National Swimmingpool Institute 1977.
≋ Swindon ☎ 0793 33404 for opening times.

The Oasis must be the most popular building in Swindon. The pool element is a fantasy structure, its half-submerged dome resembling a flying saucer, and the rectangular multi-purpose hall looks somewhat incongruous against it. Sadly the complex suffers through lack of maintenance, inevitably continuous and costly with the number of people using the facilities.

Swindon
RENAULT PARTS DISTRIBUTION CENTRE, Rivermead Estate, Westlea Down, Swindon. *Foster Associates.* 1983.
M4 to Junction 16 ≋ Swindon ☎ 0793 613421

This breathtaking building has to be one of the most remarkable ever constructed in the UK. The structure comprises an array of bright yellow steel masts supporting a lightweight membrane roof and a simple grey cladding system. The result is massive warehousing with a stunning showroom and training school. Unpopular with the locals for the way it interrupts the rural skyline, the centre has attracted designers in their droves to stare in wonder.

259

260

261

262

Swindon
WILTSHIRE RADIO BROADCASTING STUDIOS, Lime Kiln Studios, Lime Kiln, Wootton Bassett, Nr Swindon, Wilts. *Nicholas Grimshaw and Partners*. 1983.

🚗 M4 Junction 16 to Wootton Bassett 🚆 Swindon 🚌 15, 16 ☏ 0793 852277/853222

Attached to an old farmhouse, the studios and reception block are quite stunning. Six studios are contained in a structure of sand-filled grp clip-to-gether panels – a quick and cheap means of achieving excellent sound insulation. The reception area is in complete contrast – lightweight white enamelled aluminium tubes and struts dance everywhere, supporting a continuous pvc rooflight. A large electrical switchbox behind the reception desk is featured in its glass-fronted case. Sadly this detail does not work in practice, detracting from an otherwise pristine interior.

Truro
CHAPTER HALL, TRURO CATHEDRAL, Cathedral Close, Truro, Cornwall. *MWT Architects*. 1967.

Awards: Civic Trust Award 1969.

🚆 Truro

The Chapter Hall is an extension to Pearson's imposing Victorian Gothic cathedral. The Gothic character is gently echoed in the modern form and sensitive use of indigenous materials in the granite columns and slate roof. The imaginative design relies on the simple expedient of raising the Hall on four columns to the level of the cathedral nave. This achieves a striking extension, while preserving the view through the Cathedral Close on the north side.

Westonbirt
WESTONBIRT ARBORETUM VISITORS CENTRE, Tetbury, Glos. *HSTB Partnership*. 1978.

Awards: RIBA Commendation 1979; Civic Trust Award 1980; Stone Federation Award 1981.

🚗 A433 between Cirencester and Tetbury ☏ 066 66220

The pavilion and refreshment kiosk straddle outcrops of local stone, blending with the superb landscape of the arboretum. From the wood-block flooring, through the structural components and finishes to the cedar shingled roof, timber is used for the entire complex echoing the setting well.

Winscombe
BARTON CHILDREN'S HOLIDAY CAMP, Webbington, Winscombe, Avon. *Form Structures*. 1978.

Awards: Civic Trust Award 1978.

🚗 off A38 from Bristol 🚌 Queen Sq 120, 121, 122 ☏ Warden 093 484 2145

This holiday centre for underprivileged children is a fine example of low-cost, low-tech architecture. Built of salvaged materials by the Bristol-based design and build company, it has proved a great success. Needless to say, some of the fixtures and fittings have taken a hammering from the young visitors, but this does not detract from an otherwise excellent scheme.

263

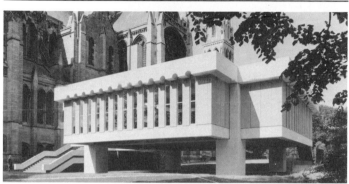

264

265

266

West Midlands

Birmingham

CENTRAL LIBRARY AND CHAMBERLAIN SQUARE, Birmingham. *The John Madin Design Group.* 1973 and 1980.

≢ Birmingham New Street

If Birmingham has a heart then this is it. The library, with roots in the Boston Civic Centre and Le Corbusier's La Tourette, is a good example of modern civic architecture. Set on the highest side of the multi-level square, it helps form the enclosure while retaining its own identity. The square acts as a foil to the elaborate Victorian and Edwardian civic buildings and a backdrop to the Chamberlain Memorial Fountain. It is a popular and pleasant place and the steps provide a convenient sitting area in the summer.

Birmingham

CLIFTON JIG AND TOOL FACTORY, Corner of Rea and McDonald Streets, Birmingham. *The Glazzard Co-operative.* 1982.

≢ Birmingham New Street

Not many Birmingham buildings show so much awareness of current architectural trends as this light engineering works. Consistent throughout in form and style, the façade is bold and imaginative. Simple utilitarian details such as downpipes and staggered windows varying the brown metal cladding and brickwork are hallmarks of its strength and energy. The building makes a good corner feature in an area otherwise devoid of any character.

Birmingham

MINING, MINERALS AND METALLURGY DEPARTMENT, Birmingham University, Pritchetts Road, Edgbaston, Birmingham. *Arup Associates.* 1965.

Award: RIBA Award 1966.

≢ Birmingham New Street

This and Casson and Conder's Department of Education opposite are good contrasting examples of architectural evolution in the 60s and 70s. The Arup building has all the hard logic typical of their best work, but is all "rationale" and no spirit. There are many notable details including the stair built around a diagonal cruciform column, and the finely detailed waffle slab, but the building somehow falls short of its true architectural potential. Outside the landscape is bare and windswept.

267

268

269

Birmingham

SIGNAL BOX, New Street Station, Birmingham. *British Rail Architect's Department*. 1967.

⇌ Birmingham New Street

This striking building is best observed from the inner ring road. With an air of Frank Lloyd Wright about it, the box combines bold horizontal and vertical shapes with a play on solid and void. Its architectural character symbolises the ingenuity and placing of the station as a whole. Although the signal box has weathered badly and is difficult to view, it must still rate as one of the best design features of any BR station.

Coventry

ARTS CENTRE, Warwick University, Coventry. *Renton Howard Wood Levin Partnership*. 1975.

Award: RIBA Award 1975.

⇌ Coventry

The scale of this building is deliberately broken down so that the mass rises from the low entrance to the flytower. Inside, levels are used again to take the visitor down from the foyer to the cafeteria and concert hall and up to the bar and auditorium. As the levels change so do the colours. The concrete blocks which dominate the structure work well inside, but tend to blend with the white and grey surroundings. In all, the building has much to offer, particularly in its spatial arrangement and three dimensional qualities.

Coventry

COVENTRY CATHEDRAL, Coventry. *Sir Basil Spence and Partners*. 1962.

⇌ Coventry

This is undoubtedly a landmark in modern British architecture. Among its fine details are the juxtaposition between the ruins of the old cathedral and the new and the pedestrian route that separates the two, ending in a square. As a home for the arts it contains Sutherland's altar tapestry, stained glass by John Piper and other major works. While the cathedral may not be favoured by the "avant-garde", it remains an important work by one of Britain's most popular post-war architects.

Coventry

WARWICK UNIVERSITY, Coventry. *YRM*. 1966–71.

Award: Library: RIBA Award 1967.

⊞ Coventry to Kenilworth Road ⇌ Coventry ⊞ 42, 43

Known for its white-tiled Modernism, Warwick University is in good shape. The detailing has lasted and the landscape has been well kept. Very much a suburban campus operating on a ring-road system, it is reminiscent of a high quality industrial estate. Some of the later buildings lack the original quality, but there are some excellent additions, notably the Psychology Department and Students' Union. Despite the social and architectural controversies surrounding their inception, few of the new universities have withstood the test of time. But Warwick maintains its architectural significance.

270

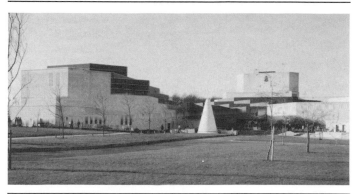

271

272

273

Yorkshire

Beverley

GLOBE MEWS HOUSING, Dog and Duck Lane, Beverley. *David Ruffle Associates*. 1982.
Award: Housing Design Award 1983.
🚗 B1230 ⇌ Beverley

Neglected for many years, this site behind the market square now sports a new private housing development. Houses are arranged around a mews court with 29 units per acre, all designed within a standard modular building envelope. But the standardisation is skillfully disguised by the mix of two and three storey homes, irregularly set to fit the site while allowing each one a back garden. The overall pattern and choice of traditional local materials gives the scheme a timeless quality.

Halifax

HALIFAX BUILDING SOCIETY HEADQUARTERS, Commercial Street, Halifax. *Building Design Partnership*. 1974.
Award: RIBA Award 1975.
🚗 off M62 junction 24 ⇌ Halifax ☎ 0422 65777

This building transcends the solution of technical problems associated with a major headquarters. The result has a quality and vigour not seen in the town since the Victorian era of Italianate mills and civic buildings. Set on an irregular sloping site, the complex has four storeys above ground level. The first two occupy only half the site, with the larger upper level supported on four service towers. Definitely of the 20th century, its spacial organisation, detailing and quality materials are reminiscent of the best American traditions, providing an envious working environment for its occupants.

Hull

THE LAWNS HALLS OF RESIDENCE, University of Hull, Harland Way, Cottingham, Hull. *Gillespie, Kidd and Coia*. 1966.
Awards: RIBA Award 1968; Civic Trust Award 1968.
🚗 B1233 ⇌ Hull 🚌 104, 105 ☎ Manager 0482 847671

Planned as a complex of 12 halls, each housing 136 undergraduates, the Lawns includes teaching and amenity buildings. Arranged around the edge of the site, each hall has its own court and is linked to its neighbours to form an undulating wall enclosing a landscaped park. Only six halls have been built to date, but the complex still looks complete. The mellow rustic brick façades of the three-storey blocks are heavily articulated, each unit expressed by a deeply recessed balcony. Groups of rooms are expressed as changes in plane and bear the same residential character of Cottingham village itself.

274

275

276

Leeds
CHANCELLOR'S COURT, University Precinct, Woodhouse Lane, Leeds 2.
Chamberlin, Powell and Bon. 1972.
Award: RIBA Award 1972.
🚗 A660 ⇌ Leeds 🚌 1, 4 ☎ Bursar's secretary 0532 431751

The 1960 development plan engendered a remarkably open urban university with a series of interrelated courts stepping down the hillside. Chancellors Court forms the new focus to the complex. Surrounded on three sides by department buildings and the senior common room, the fourth side is defined by a high-level walkway connected to the ingeniously planned lecture theatre block. The whole campus makes a convincing statement about urban design as conceived in the 50s and 60s.

Leeds
POTTERNEWTON GARDENS HOUSING, Henconner Lane, Chapel Allerton, Leeds 7. *Yorkshire Development Group.* 1973.
Awards: DoE Housing Award 1975; RIBA Award 1976.
🚗 off A61 ⇌ Leeds 🚌 6, 22

This small infill estate of high density, low rise housing is in a densely populated urban area of predominantly terraced housing. Existing street patterns have been retained and the scheme focuses on a central pedestrian court. The rigorous layout and scale of the design maintains the grain of the urban fabric. The range of dwellings includes two-storey houses and flats and patio bungalows, each with an open entrance court and private garden. Detailing is simple and consistent and with the newly mature planting the estate provides a residential environment excellent of its kind.

Leeds
TOWN STREET HOUSING DEVELOPMENT, Chapel Allerton, Leeds 7.
Leeds Corporation Housing Department. 1970.
Award: DoE Housing Award 1971.
⇌ Leeds 🚌 6, 22

Replacing derelict 18th-century houses in this old West Riding village, Town Street is an early example of the changing attitude to infill housing manifested in the 70s. The original line of the street has been retained, but transformed into a pedestrian route with central paved walkway and compacted gravel margins. Opening off the street at a slight angle, the housing gives way in places to well proportioned squares. With its dark rustic brickwork, punctuated by deeply recessed openings, and blue slate monopitch roofs, the scheme is simple, homogeneous, yet full of visual interest.

Richmond
RICHMONDSHIRE SWIMMING POOL, Station Road, Richmond, North Yorkshire. *Napper, Errington, Collerton Partnership.* 1976.
Awards: Structural Steel Design Award 1976; RIBA Award 1977; Civic Trust Award 1978.
🚗 A1/A6136 ☎ 0748 4581

Though clearly of its own time, this building, in an outstanding conservation area and adjacent to the restored old railway station, complements its historic setting, largely through careful use of levels on the sloping site. The predominant features are the three visually independent hipped roofs, each supported by two diagonally braced pairs of columns. A fine curtain of double glazing forms the walls allowing views in and out of the pool.

277

278

279

280

Sheffield
CRUCIBLE THEATRE, Arundel Gate, Sheffield. *Renton Howard Wood Associates.* 1972.
Award: RIBA Award 1972.
⇌ Sheffield ☎ Administrator 0742 760621

Occupying a central site at the edge of the civic development area, the complex comprises a 1,000-seat auditorium and 300-seat studio theatre served by common foyers and workshops. The octagonal auditorium provides the dominant motif, its 180-raked seating focusing on a stepped promontary stage. The main foyer and bar spiral around five sides of the auditorium in a series of interlocking spaces. Here fair-faced concrete and brightly coloured fittings create a suitable impact. Externally the white concrete blockwork is withstanding the ravages of the industrial environment remarkably well.

Sheffield
PARK HILL HOUSING, Duke Street/South Street, Sheffield. *Sheffield Corporation Architect's Department.* 1960.
Award: DoE Good Design in Housing Award 1967.
⇌ Sheffield

Unquestionably one of Britain's most significant housing schemes, Park Hill incorporates architectural and sociological ideas that had fermented over the previous decade. The first expressions were the "street-deck" projects entered by the Smithsons and Ling and Smith in the 1952 Golden Lane competition. At Park Hill the street-deck idea is tailored to the site to appear inevitable. By contrast, the nearby Hyde Park scheme, built in 1966 using the same vocabulary, appears self-consciously picturesque.

York
THEATRE ROYAL, St Leonards, York. *Patrick Gwynne.* 1967.
🚌 A64 ⇌ York ☎ 0904 58162

Despite its rich historic core, York is singularly lacking in good 20th-century buildings, this extension being a rare exception. A new entrance, foyer, restaurant and bars have been grafted on to the Victorian Gothic building. Hexagonal-headed mushroom columns support the roof and floors, giving a consistent structural theme. The upper floors float free of surrounding walls, while the ground floor has split levels to separate various functions. The external wall of the old theatre is used inside the new block to great effect, and the new glazed external walls allow the sculptured interior to be part of the street scene.

York
UNIVERSITY OF YORK, Heslington, York. *Robert Matthew Johnson-Marshall and Partners.* 1968.
🚌 A1079 ⇌ York 🚌 7,16

In its superb landscaped setting, York, more than any other post-war university, has the atmosphere of the American campus. Organised on a collegiate basis, it has no identifiable faculty buildings as such. Each college contains formal and informal teaching spaces, with only the science labs, main auditorium and library occupying separate blocks. Most of the buildings are constructed using the CLASP system. Within this discipline the architects have produced an extraordinary variety of layout and an unpretentious architecture which is relaxed and informal.

281

282

283

284

Scotland

Airdrie
BSC IMPERIAL WORKS ADMINISTRATIVE AND AMENITY BUILDINGS, Victoria Place, Airdrie, Strathclyde. *Reiach, Hall, Blyth Partnership.* 1977. Awards: RIBA Award 1978; Structural Steel Design Commendation 1978. ≽ Airdrie ☎ Manager 02364 54561

Two separate buildings add a sleek refinement to an industry not noted for the quality of its working environment. Naturally, steel was specified in the brief. The result is a cheerful but restful environment, with bright colours and the exposed ductwork as the most eye-catching features. The administration building steps elegantly up the hill with pleasing internal spaces created by the changes of level. Problems with a leaking roof and inadequate temperature control have made staff contemptuous of the RIBA Award and new additions such as the external doors are beginning to jar on the whole.

Cardross
ST PETER'S COLLEGE, Cardross. *Gillespie, Kidd and Coia.* 1966. Award: RIBA Award 1967.
≙⃝ A814

St Peter's College is a tragedy. Now unused, it is in an advanced state of decay. Approached via a long drive it stands precipitously on the edge of a ravine. Despite the dereliction, the composition, particularly of the remarkable refectory and chapel spaces created by the inward cantilevering of the dormitory block, gives a unity to the different activities of the former seminary. The culmination of this space in a top-lit altar is masterful. A complex knuckle of pedestrian routes forms the link to the teaching block which cantilevers dramatically over the ravine.

Cumbernauld
KILDRUM PARISH CHURCH, Cumbernauld. *Alan Reiach and Partners.* 1965.
≽ Glasgow, then bus from station

One of the few distinguished buildings in the New Town, the complex comprises two rectangular boxes – the kirk with its concrete bell tower and a parish hall with a low lying manse behind. A timber-lined steel roof is supported on slender timber-clad steel columns, and floats over an undulating clerestory. At one point the clerestory dips to the floor to reveal from the inside the altar cross placed outside in a walled garden. Though the brickwork has spalled badly and the parish hall has suffered vandalism, the whole composition remains one of elegance and restraint.

285

286

287

Dundee
DUNDEE REPERTORY THEATRE, Tay Square, Dundee. *Nicoll Russell.* 1982.

≈ Dundee ☎ 0382 27684

Built for £1.2 million, this cleverly planned building includes an auditorium for 490 with audience and backstage facilities. The main source of enjoyment is the almost fanatical thoroughness in the inventive detailing of the simple concrete block and stained timber construction. A small, but complex, glazed foyer expands dramatically into Tay Square via a "grand staircase". The strong geometry of the auditorium is rigorously expressed in the main elevation, while inside the concrete blocks are sculpted to cradle the seating and divide the audience space.

Dundee
OLIVETTI OFFICES, Dryburg Industrial Estate, Dundee. *Edward Cullinan Architects.* 1972.

Award: Financial Times Industrial Building Award.

🚗 off A923 ≈ Dundee ☎ Property Section 01-785 6666

Typical of Cullinan's schemes, the section is the key to this building. Covered parking and workshops at ground level are dominated by first floor offices. A great orange roof hovers over piloti sheltering the walls and providing clerestory lighting. Expansion was planned with this building wrapping around two sides of an imaginary courtyard. In the event, the company has contracted to three directors instead of the 50 envisaged. Though the low level of roof insulation has dogged performance, this remains a novel design, with flexible yet structured offices and a strong corporate image.

East Kilbride
ST BRIDE'S ROMAN CATHOLIC CHURCH, Plathorn Drive, East Kilbride. *Gillespie, Kidd and Coia.* 1965.

Award: RIBA Bronze Medal 1963.

≈ East Kilbride

A suitably massive scale allows this church to assert itself in a rather fragmented new town landscape. A huge red brick box, free standing campanile (now badly spalled) and a low-lying complex of parish rooms and priests' house combine around a pleasant square. Inside the general impression is dark and heavy, but enjoyment comes from the way the deep brick skin is modulated to let in light and accommodate a dramatic spiral staircase and folded to mark the entrance. A free-standing gallery set to one side cleverly defines the Lady Chapel and separates the main space from the administrative areas.

Edinburgh
DISTILLERS COMPANY PLC HEADQUARTERS OFFICE, Ellersley Road, Edinburgh 12. *Robert Matthew Johnson-Marshall and Partners.* 1984.

🚗 A8 to Corstorphine ≈ Haymarket

This scheme promises to be a dignified and harmonious addition to Edinburgh's western suburbs. Development restrictions and environmental considerations produced a low stepped section amphitheatrical form. Catering facilities are at the base and directors' suites at the top. The intermediate offices are cellular, perimeter dependent and fully air conditioned. External materials are York sandstone and lead fascias. Inside the planning grid is emphasised by bays of "egg-crate" ceiling with acrylic finished steel partitions between.

288

289

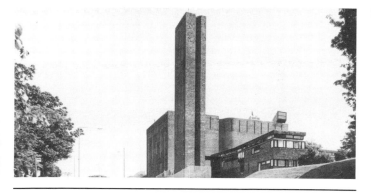

290

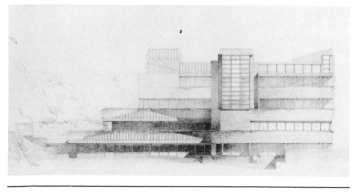

291

Edinburgh
LYNEDOCH HOUSE SHELTERED HOUSING, 23 Lynedoch Place, Edinburgh. *Roland Wedgwood Associates.* 1979.
Awards: Saltire Society Award for Housing in Scotland 1979. RIBA Award 1980.
🚌 left off A90 past Randolph Crescent ⇌ Edinburgh ☎ Warden 031-225 3999

   The significance of this design lies in its contribution to the site on the southern lip of the steep Leith Valley. The drama is intensified by the cliff-like rear tenement elevations. Comprising 22 single and double units plus warden's flat, the scheme emerges from behind a high stone wall and ascends to a lively skyline of canted corner details and eyrie-like conservatory. The three-storey end house of the adjacent terrace is incorporated into the design, old and new being linked by the pyramid-roofed dining area.

Edinburgh
MORTONHALL CREMATORIUM, Howdenhall, Edinburgh. *Sir Basil Spence, Glover and Ferguson.* 1967.
🚌 Galashiels Road from Edinburgh 🚌 42 from Edinburgh ⇌ Edinburgh ☎ 031-664 4314

   Sited in a hollow at the edge of a wood, the crematorium with its two chapels merges unobtrusively into the landscape. The white aggregate block has worn well and gives a sharp definition to the angled forms of the chapels seen against the trees.

Edinburgh
THE NEW CLUB, 85 Princes Street, Edinburgh. *Reiach and Hall.* 1976.
⇌ Edinburgh ☎ 031-226 4881

   Entirely financed by the ground floor retail space, the new club replaces the 1834 listed original. The division between club and shops is emphasised by the horizontal sweep of the first floor deck, the club itself starting at second-storey level. The granite clad elevation is rather hard and out of scale with the street, but inside the atmosphere has been re-created with finesse. While sympathetic to its users, the design is uncompromisingly of its time. But it is wearing extremely well and is worth persistent effort to get inside.

Edinburgh
NEW GLASSHOUSES, Royal Botanic Gardens, Inverleith Row or Arboretum Road, Edinburgh. *Ministry of Public Building and Works.* 1965.
🚌 8, 9, 19, 23 or 27 from city centre ⇌ Edinburgh ☎ 031-552 7171

   Following the Victorian engineering tradition for innovation and daring, the new glasshouses have more in common with the adjacent 1850s palm houses than their more recent portal frame shed neighbours. A light tetrahedron and high tensile structure provide a clear internal space divided into a number of hot houses. A separate small orchid house provides a link to existing glass houses. While this scheme contributes to the richness of its surroundings the extension to the adjacent Modern Art Gallery sadly falls down in this respect.

292

293

294

295

Edinburgh
NUFFIELD TRANSPLANTATION SURGERY UNIT, Western General Hospital, Crewe Road, Edinburgh. *Peter Womersley*. 1968.
Award: Bayer International Award. 1964.
🚃 17, 19, 47 ⇌ Edinburgh ☏ 031-332 2525
  Though now badly stained, this remains by far the most memorable post-war hospital building in Scotland, establishing a slightly eccentric presence through its playful use of form. The sculptural concrete creates an exaggerated motif throughout the complex, with the entrance in the link between new and existing a composition of glass and concrete structural elements. Beyond, but very private, are a ward for six patients, two operating theatres and offices.

Edinburgh
ROYAL COMMONWEALTH POOL, Dalkeith Road, Edinburgh. *Robert Matthew Johnson-Marshall and Partners*. 1970.
Awards: RIBA Award 1970; Structural Steel Design Award 1970; Civic Trust Award 1972.
⇌ Edinburgh ☏ 031-667 7211
  This unpretentious yet elegant complex is principally distinguished by its internal legibility and use of the site. The strong horizontal line contrasts with Arthur's Seat behind and Spence's nearby Scottish Widows Building. Externally, the low lying complex exudes an air of civic importance appropriate to its occasional international role. Inside, the main pool uses the natural fall of the site and is placed at a lower level beyond the entrance. In these days of exotic plastic leisure centres, the dignified restraint of this design is a lasting relief.

Edinburgh
ROYAL MAIL HOUSE SORTING OFFICE, 10 Brunswick Road, Edinburgh. *Sir Basil Spence, Glover and Ferguson*. 1982.
⇌ Edinburgh ☏ Head Post Office 031-550 8232
  Set in a featureless area surrounded by demolition sites, this building is an elegant and jolly addition to the city skyline. A blockwork ground floor forms the base for an aluminium-clad sorting shed which is raised on piloti and culminates in three distinctive chimneys. The massing falls away from the entrance in a series of interlocking low pitched roofs to a low loading bay. In between, the façades are modelled by staircases descending from the first floor. The whole composition is enlivened by thorough details inside and out picked out appropriately in pillar box red.

Edinburgh
SCOTTISH PROVIDENT INSTITUTION HEAD OFFICE PHASE 2, 8 St Andrew Square, Edinburgh. *Rowand Anderson, Kininmonth and Paul*. 1968.
⇌ Edinburgh ☏ 031-556 9181
  Undoubtedly the finest new building in the New Town, this block provides offices for 300 staff, with boardroom, roof-top restaurant and basement car-park. The main elevation to the square is an excellent composition of solids and voids, horizontals and verticals, culminating in a glazed box and service tower. The entrance hall gives sight into the large open-plan central office and boardroom. The deep plan building emerges again on South St David Street with a quieter largely horizontal façade. Construction is of reinforced concrete with Italian granite cladding and aluminium framed toughened glazing.

296

297

298

299

Edinburgh
THE SCOTTISH WIDOWS FUND AND LIFE ASSURANCE SOCIETY HEAD OFFICES, Dalkeith Road, Edinburgh. *Sir Basil Spence, Glover and Ferguson.* 1976.
Award: RIBA Award 1977.
🚌 2, 14, 21, 33, 36, 49, to Jedburgh ⇌ Edinburgh ☎ Premises Manager 031-655 6000

A series of brown glazed interlocking hexagons of varying heights occupies an open site. The seemingly casual way the hexagons have been massed is a little disquieting, though the planning absurdities inherent in their form have been avoided. The entrance is particularly exciting, the route crossing a reflecting pool into an airy foyer. Notable too is the well disguised two-storey car park set beneath a roof garden.

Edinburgh
SHELTERED HOUSING, 9–11 Cameron Crescent, Edinburgh. *Nicholas Groves-Raines.* 1983.
🚌 7, 37, 33, 36, 42, 14, 2, 21 ⇌ Edinburgh ☎ Viewpoint Housing Association 031-556 1676

Unlike many of its contemporaries, this 43-unit scheme, while acknowledging the nearby tenements, has not allowed architectural good manners to stifle a courageous and controversial new design. Though it honours the scale and colours of the tenements, the dominant features are decidedly not of Edinburgh. The brickwork patterning is reminiscent of English Victorian industrial architecture while the windows have a 30s horizontality to them. Exposed staircases at either end have oriental proportions and link the flats to adjacent housing which also forms part of the development.

Edinburgh
UNIVERSITY OF EDINBURGH LIBRARY, George Square, Edinburgh. *Sir Basil Spence, Glover and Ferguson.* 1967.
Awards: RIBA Award 1968; Civic Commendation 1969.
⇌ Edinburgh ☎ University Estates Department 031-667 1011

This library and the adjacent theatre are the only buildings of merit to emerge from the architectural carnage of George Square. The graceful horizontality of the cantilevered balconies is equally apparent viewed from the square itself or across the meadows to the south. The interior is simply arranged, a double-height enquiry lobby leading to circulation cores with functional spaces above. Most areas have outside views. A podium containing the two lower floors sets the building apart, giving it an appropriate sense of importance within the square.

Galashiels
STUDIO FOR BERNAT KLEIN DESIGN, Nr Galashiels, Borders Region. *Peter Womersley.* 1972.
Awards: RIBA Award 1973; Edinburgh Architectural Association Centenary Medal 1973.
🚌 leave Selkirk for Galashiels, studio is on left about 3 miles out ☎ 0750 20730

The idea of transparent boxes in a wooded setting is not new, but here Womersley has broken from Miesian antecedents to create a dynamic building with its own presence. Designed as a textiles showroom and studio, it features reinforced concrete edge beams forming strongly expressed horizontals against the vertical of the blue brick services core. Complete 360-degree glazing offers wonderful views from both floors, while the roof doubles as a terrace.

300

301

302

303

Glasgow
THE BURRELL COLLECTION MUSEUM, Pollok Park, Glasgow. *Barry Gasson Architects*. 1983.

🚗 A77 from city centre to Pollokshaws and Pollok Country Park 🚌 21, 23, 44, 48 or 57 from Glasgow

The result of a competition for a museum to house a diverse art collection, this is one of Scotland's best post-war buildings. Selecting a site hard against a corner of woodland to the north, the architects have created a series of spaces that relate dramatically to the surrounding landscape. To the north, a superb cool high gallery merges through a glass and stainless steel wall into adjacent woodland, while to the east and south more expansive two-storey spaces look out across the meadow. These larger perimeter galleries enclose smaller, more intimate spaces. Medieval doorways from the collection are integrated into the scheme.

Glasgow
CHURCH OF OUR LADY OF GOOD COUNSEL, Craigpark, Dennistoun, Glasgow. *Gillespie, Kidd and Coia*. 1964.
Award: RIBA Award 1966.

🚗 M8 then A8 🚆 Glasgow

The dramatic roof dominates the design, its asymmetry generated by a trapezoid plan rising to its highest point above the altar. A slow ascent from the external area above the street level via the porch to a rising stair inside gives dignity to the entrance route. Six squat interior columns add to the massive feeling of the roof, which is lined with stained redwood and lit naturally through a band of windows on either side. A gallery has been set to one side concealing the sacristy and confessionals beneath and creating more intimate spaces for the Lady Chapel and baptistry.

Inverness
EDEN COURT THEATRE, Bishop's Road, Inverness. *Law and Dunbar-Naismith*. 1976.
Award: RIBA Commendation 1977.

🚆 Inverness ☎ Director 0463 239841

The main external components of this 800-seat theatre are the massive precast concrete flytowers and cluster of hexagonal roofs to the foyer. The contrast between the two is perhaps a little unhappy as the building cannot decide whether it is grand or folksy; but inside the roofs come into their own, concealing a spacially complex foyer. The foyer itself rises through three floors, giving access to all levels of the auditorium. Here a proscenium arch faces stalls surrounded by a pleasing geometry of staggered boxes. For such a grand space, the internal finishes are a little dull.

Irvine New Town
GIRDLE TOLL HOUSING, PHASE 3, Irvine New Town, Ayrshire. *Irvine Development Corporation*. 1976.

🚗 A736 from Glasgow, right at Stanecastle Roundabout 🚌 from Irvine to Bourtreehill 🚆 Irvine ☎ Chief Accountant/Planner 0294 214100

The greatest joy of this scheme is the network of pedestrian routes designed to provide a variety of enclosures and visual experiences. The estate itself is much larger than it seems. Set opposite the soon-to-be restored Stane Castle Tower House, and entered through a fine Victorian stone archway it consists in the main of one-, two- and three-storey white rendered houses with darkened window surrounds and monopitch roofs. Vehicular access is restricted to culs-de-sac penetrating the development at various points.

304

305

306

307

Killichonan

PRIVATE HOUSE, Gianon, Killichonan, Loch Rannoch, Tayside. *Reiach and Hall.* 1968.

B846 ☎ Reiach and Hall 031-225 8444

Sitting on a slight promontory surrounded by trees, the main living space of this retirement home offers superb views. The low lying exterior is partly hidden, while inside the plan is dominated by a split level living/dining/entrance space. Here, blue brick perimeter seating merges to form the hearth of a free-standing chimney. The design is simple, clean and economical and though very much of its era, clearly long lasting. Not only has it endured the rigours of the Highland climate, but has successfully predicted and accommodated the Danish clients' lifestyle.

Killin

BEN LAWERS MOUNTAIN VISITOR CENTRE, Ben Lawers, Nr Killin, Perthshire. *Moira and Moira (now Betty L.C. Moira Architects).* 1973.

A827 from Killin along north side of Loch Tay, then towards Glen Lyon and Bridge of Balgie (road may be impassable or dangerous in winter) ☎ Warden 031-226 5922

This small visitors centre perched up high under Ben Lawers is an exemplar of how to build contextually without resorting to a phoney vernacular. The stone base with its curiously shaped timber superstructure is reminiscent of a gun emplacement and in spite of the harsh Highlands climate shows no signs of decay. The practice is no stranger to detailing for extreme climatic conditions having also completed a mountaintop observation restaurant in the Cairngorms.

Perth

COMMERCIAL STREET HOUSING, Perth. *James Parr and Partners.* 1978. Awards: Perth Civic Trust Commendation 1978; Institute National du Logement Prix International d'Architecture Commendation 1978; Saltire Society Award 1980; Civic Trust Award 1980: Ambrose Congreve Commendation 1980; Cembureau European Award 1982.

A85 towards Dundee ⇌ Perth

A clear hit with residents, this is the most photogenic post-war housing scheme in Scotland. Two uncompromisingly modern blocks are carefully massed with two individual houses placed against the main mass to define a delightful riverside walk. Materials – sand-blasted pink concrete blocks, second hand slates and stained timber – are carefully controlled and simply detailed. Flashes of red occur on doors and handrails. The scheme works equally well from a distance or as a route through.

Redgarton

COUNTRYSIDE COMMISSION FOR SCOTLAND HEADQUARTERS VISITORS CENTRE, Battleby House, Redgarton, Perthshire. *Morris and Steedman.* 1974.

Awards: RIBA Award 1974; Heritage Year Award 1975.

A9 north of Perth ☎ 0738 27921

An example of high quality conversion work and new-build, Battleby is worth a visit for its architecture and for the work of the landscape centre itself. The new circular auditorium is hidden by two austere stone halls, linked and converted into a generous foyer and exhibition space. The glory of the windowless auditorium is its roof, which has the sort of elegant structural functionalism that restores faith in the "form follows function" ethic. A magnificent lattice of steel and timber elements forms a three dimensional truss to support a timber-lined dome.

308

309

310

311

St Andrews
ANDREW MELVILLE HALL, ST ANDREWS UNIVERSITY, North Haugh, St Andrews, Fife. *James Stirling*. 1968.

🚌 to St Andrews from Leuchars 🚊 Leuchars ☎ Domestic Bursar 0334 74437

This dramatic gesture has two "finger" residence blocks reaching out to sea. The 250 single rooms have a slightly amorphous plan resulting from a geometry which articulates each room on the exterior. The entrance plunges dramatically down the hillside to the central facilities block which is a slight disappointment. The finely ribbed concrete on the residences has weathered well, but some glazing and the entrance area generally are showing signs of wear. The halls are unpopular with students, possibly because of their peripheral location rather than any overbearing quality of the architecture.

Shotts
CUMMINS ENGINE FACTORY, Shottskirk Road, Shotts, Lanarkshire. *Ahrends Burton and Koralek*. 1983.

Award: Structural Steel Design Award 1983.

🚌 M8 junction 5 🚊 Glasgow or Edinburgh ☎ 0501 20291

Typical of Cummins architectural patronage, this is Scotland's finest post-war industrial scheme. A complex design incorporates an existing building now converted into open plan offices, an assembly line with raised walkways leading to the workers' car park set on a terrace to the north, and top-lit work spaces. The demountable perimeter wall is defined as a separate undulating structure which, with high-level walkways, gives the complex its main character. The existing north-lit factory has been brilliantly disguised externally by recladding in aluminium with "saw-tooth" fenestration, and inside by clever use of colour.

Stirling
PRINCIPAL'S HOUSE, UNIVERSITY OF STIRLING, Airthray, Stirling. *Morris and Steedman*. 1967.

🚌 off A9 to Bridge of Allan ☎ 0786 3171

This house makes dramatic use of its site, forming a boundary where a flat hill top meets a steep wooded slope. Broadly L-shaped, the plan contains the public rooms in the corner of the L with family and guest bedrooms in the two wings. Access is via a partially glazed route fronting a courtyard. The elevation to the court is low lying, horizontal and neutral, in contrast to the expansive elevation on the opposite side.

Stirling
UNIVERSITY OF STIRLING, Stirling. *Robert Matthew Johnson-Marshall and Partners*. 1974.

Awards: Pathfoot Building: Civic Trust Award 1968; RIBA Award 1969. Halls of residence: Concrete Society Commendation 1971. Phase 1: RIBA Commendation 1973.

🚌 M9 then Bridge of Allan Road 🚊 Stirling 🚌 to Bridge of Allan from Stirling ☎ 0786 3171

The university is arranged around a lake in a sort of academic arcadia, the buildings pulled back in a bowl of mature trees. Across the footbridge are the residences, their horizontal lines stepping down towards the lake. The arts centre, library and teaching block are grouped together, with the Pathfoot Building set slightly apart. The use of similar materials and strong horizontals knits the whole together.

312

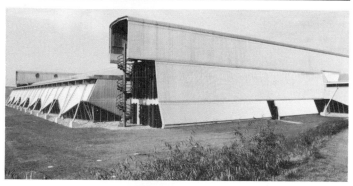

313

314

315

Ulster

Belfast
BEARNAGH GLEN SHELTERED HOUSING, Glen Road, Andersonstown, Belfast 11. *Northern Ireland Housing Executive.* 1982.
🚌 Glen Road bus from city centre 🚆 Belfast 🕿 James Butcher Housing Association 0232 225175

This scheme exploits a difficult steeply sloping site, taking advantage of the restricted access to create a sense of enclosure. The seclusion is enhanced by cloistered courtyards and covered walkways linking the houses to the shared facility block. Ramps help with difficult slopes. Materials are suitably domestic and the mottled clay brick facing and stained timberwork are relatively maintenance free.

Belfast
NORTHERN BANK HEAD OFFICE, Donegall Square West, Belfast. *Building Design Partnership.* 1976.
Award: RIBA Award 1977.
🚆 Belfast 🕿 0232 245277

In the view of the RIBA assessors, this building "successfully achieves the difficult task of emphatically stating its importance as housing a major financial and commercial headquarters while not challenging the dominance of the City Hall nor adding another strident note". The Portland stone cladding and bronze tinted glazing have weathered well, largely because of the care in detailing. Inside, the open plan incorporates many special features, such as an air conditioning heat reclaim system and low percentage glazing to assist environmental control.

Belfast
ROYAL ULSTER AGRICULTURAL SOCIETY MEMBERS' ROOMS, Lisburn Road, Balmoral, Belfast. *Ferguson & McIlveen.* 1965.
Award: Civic Trust Award (Class 1) 1966.
🚌 from Belfast to Lisburn on main road 🚆 Belfast 🚌 Citybus from Belfast city centre 🕿 The RUAS Chief Executive Belfast 665225

The requirement was for a building to provide full permanent amenities for members of the Society, particularly at the annual Agricultural Show, which would be versatile enough to accommodate other functions. The hall spans 62 ft in both directions and is of in-situ reinforced concrete. The rear block is of in-situ column and beam construction in a simple form to act as a suitable foil to the octagonal Hall. The Civic Trust Award assessor commented: "The building possesses the simplicity and inevitability of all 'thoroughbred' works of architecture."

316

317

318

Belfast
ULSTER MUSEUM EXTENSION, Stranmillis Road, Belfast. *Francis Pym and Chief Architect's Branch Ministry of Finance.* 1972.
≱ Belfast ☎ 0232 668251
Originally designed in 1911 by J.C. Wynne, the Ulster Museum has been extended twice. The most recent scheme incorporates some of the Classical features of the original façade melting gradually into a boldly sculptural concrete composition. Inside the galleries ascend in a helical arrangement producing a series of dramatically varied spaces to take the art treasures.

Craigavon
PORTADOWN NEW TECHNICAL COLLEGE, 26 Lurgan Road, Portadown, Craigavon, Co Armagh. *Shanks Leighton Kennedy and FitzGerald.* 1976.
M1 from Belfast to Portadown. College is 1 mile outside Portadown on Portadown-Lurgan interchange road ≱ Belfast Ulsterbus from Belfast ☎ The Secretary, Portadown 37111
This multi-level group of buildings is situated in a large campus. The heart of the complex is the Technical College and Assembly Hall, with the Junior High School, technical workshops and gymnasium blocks arranged round it. Their relationship with each other, and with the main building, sustain an ascending spatial sequence of surprise and complexity.

Dungannon
DUNGANNON DISTRICT COUNCIL HEADQUARTERS, Circular Road, Dungannon, Co Tyrone. *Shanks Leighton Kennedy & FitzGerald.* 1978. Award: RIBA Commendation 1980.
M1 from Belfast to Dungannon, within the town boundary on Circular Road ≱ Belfast Ulsterbus from Belfast city centre ☎ The Town Clerk, Dungannon 25311
Dungannon reflects the formality of 18th-century town planning. Over the past 10 years it has been scarred by bombing, but much of its late Georgian building stock survives. The design of this building makes full use of its setting, and its geometry is a response to the configuration of the sloping site. The use of a local red clay brick emphasises its indigenous quality.

Holywood
ULSTER FOLK AND TRANSPORT MUSEUM, Cultra, Co Down. *Ferguson and McIlveen.* 1980.
Award: RIBA Award 1983.
off Belfast to Bangor road ☎ 023 17 5411
The brief called for a gallery capable of sub-division into three distinct exhibition areas with a design linking the interior and exterior area. The resulting building comprises four elements on different levels of the sloping site with tall glazed links between. Dark green porcelain enamelled steel-faced panels form contrasting solid areas. These were chosen to complement the vernacular building exhibits, while receding into the backdrop of the heavily wooded surroundings. A visit to this building is a must for any visitor to Ulster.

319

320

321

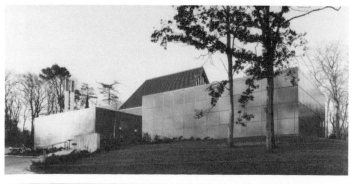

322

Wales

Aberdare

LLWYDCOED CREMATORIUM, Aberdare, Mid Glamorgan. *Burgess and Partners.* 1971.
Award: RIBA Award 1971.
🚗 A465 ☎ Superintendent 0685 874115

This is an exceptionally fine structure which appears to have grown out of an inner core. It is, in fact, a tightly disciplined arrangement of three chapels and open wreath courts. Indigenous materials such as stone, slate and white render help the complex harmonise with the moorland landscape.

Aberystwyth

UNIVERSITY GREAT HALL AND HUGH OWEN BUILDING, Penglais, Aberystwyth, Dyfed. *Percy Thomas Partnership.* 1970, 1975.
Awards: Great Hall: Royal National Eisteddfod Gold Medal 1971; Civic Trust Award 1971; RIBA Award 1972. Hugh Owen Building: RIBA Commendation 1977; SCONUL Design Award 1978; Royal National Eisteddfod Gold Medal 1979.
🚗 A487 ⇌ Aberystwyth ☎ 0970 3177

Since the early 70s Aberystwyth has been the most exciting of the Welsh universities. The Great Hall forms the nucleus of a harmonious building complex, providing a visual reference point. Though grand in conception and monumental in character, there is a sense of intimacy inside. Despite its volume, this building is kept to the scale of the complex.

Caernarfon

HAFAN ELAN HOUSING ESTATE, Llanrug, nr Caernarfon, Gwynedd. *Bowen Dann Davies Partnership.* 1979.
Awards: Civic Trust Commendation 1980; Welsh Office Housing Medal 1980; Royal National Eisteddfod Gold Medal 1982; RIBA Commendation 1982.
🚗 off A4086 🚌 Crossville Bus from Caernarfon ☎ Warden 0286 5600

The low, long form of the 24 bungalows and the sensitive layout comprising two irregular courts and a narrow pedestrian street give this development an intimacy and warmth that is all too rare in modern housing estates. Steep slate roofs and rough stone boundary walls reinforce the character and "tie" it to the earth in a seemingly natural way. The dwellings belong here as much as the farmsteads and quarrymen's cottages of this part of Wales.

323

324

325

Cardiff
AMERSHAM INTERNATIONAL LABORATORIES, Forest Farm Industrial Estate, Whitchurch, Cardiff. *Percy Thomas Partnership*. 1980.
Awards: RIBA Award 1982; Financial Times Architect at Work Award 1982. Concrete Society Commendation.
🚗 M4/A470 junction 30 🚉 Radyr ☎ 0222 515858

At first sight this sophisticated complex resembles an educational institution, with only the 50 m high ventilation shafts indicating the industrial use for the manufacture of radioisotopes. Extensive use of high-tech materials such as glass reinforced plastic panels and reflective solar glazing and the curved design suggest the clinical laboratory environment. A long spinal corridor links laboratories and stores to the circular amenity and administrative block. Future expansion is anticipated along the south side of the spine.

Cardiff
CROWN OFFICES, Cathays Park, Cardiff. *Alex Gordon Partnership*. 1980.
🚗 north of main shopping centre 🚉 Cardiff

Considering its size, this fortress-like building fits in well with the civic centre complex, sharing the same Portland stone finish. Its mass is cleverly reduced by stepping the façade back above and below the projecting third floor. Thus the lower floors, set behind a colonnade of rectangular pillars, appear as a single storey, the second floor is sealed down to look like a mezzanine and the copper-clad upper floors seem to be part of the roof.

Cardiff
DEPARTMENT OF MUSIC, UNIVERSITY COLLEGE, Corbett Road, Cardiff. *Alex Gordon Partnership*. 1970.
🚗 nothern end of Civic Centre 🚉 Cardiff ☎ Buildings officer 0222 44211

Careful choice of materials and excellent detailing help this self-effacing red brick building to fit in with its Victorian, Jacobean, and Gothic style neighbours. Sited on the edge of Cathays Park, it acts as a foil to the white Portland stone civic buildings opposite. A Hepworth sculpture marks the separate public entrance to the 400-seat rehearsal hall contained within the structure.

Cardiff
ST DAVID'S CONCERT AND CONFERENCE HALL, Working Street, Cardiff. *The Seymour Harris Partnership*. 1982.
🚉 Cardiff ☎ Director 0222 42611

Built on a confined city centre site, this building appears to be detached from its surroundings, access being by way of a complex and confusing system of stairs and escalators leading up above two storeys of shops. The foyers and lounges form interesting interior spaces, while the 2,000-seat auditorium bears a superficial resemblance to Scharoun's Berlin Philharmonie. Visibility is excellent and acoustics good, but the open cell ceiling exposing the servicing is visually disconcerting until the lights are dimmed. Light colours give the interior a distinctly cool feeling.

326

327

328

329

Cardiff
WELSH FOLK MUSEUM, St Fagans, Cardiff. *Percy Thomas Partnership.*
1968–81.
Award: Royal National Eisteddfod Gold Medal 1978.
🚗 off A48 or A4119 🚌 32 from Cardiff 🚆 Cardiff 🕾 Curator 0222
569441

The problem facing the architects was to fit a large public building into
a well established folk park without destroying the re-created rural setting.
The sloping site helped in that galleries could be staggered with two-storey
units facing the car park and main entrance. The galleries spiral up around
an open court with a pool with ramps linking the different levels. The reinforced concrete frame is exposed inside the building and clad with light
grey bricks outside. This makes a rather harsh exterior, but the interior
works well.

Cardiff
WELSH INDUSTRIAL AND MARITIME MUSEUM, Bute Street, Cardiff.
Burgess and Partners. 1977.
Award: Cardiff 2000 Civic Society Award.
🚌 9 from city centre 🚆 Cardiff 🕾 Curator 0222 371805

The striking Miesian red brick exterior is simple and well detailed with
sloping plinths and a deep overhanging glazed roof supported on steel
stanchions. The interior is a veritable hall of power, its exposed roof structure, engine-house windows, open wells and bold exhibits being stun-
ningly appropriate. Extensions are planned to treble the size of the building
in due course.

Newport
DUFFRYN HOUSING ESTATE, Newport, Gwent. *MacCormac and
Jamieson, Wales and West Design Group.* 1979.
Award: RIBA Award 1980.
🚗 M4 junction 28 🚆 Newport 🚌 15

Comprising 1,000 homes, this is one of the largest and most exciting examples of perimeter housing in Britain. Most of the dwellings have
monopitch roofs with brick and asbestos external cladding. Wooden balconies create interest at first floor level. Though from the road the homes
appear identical the back view gives a more varied picture and a large triangular wood at the heart of the site relieves monotony. The development includes a primary school, but unfortunately economic cuts prevented the
proposed district centre from being built.

Newport
INMOS MICROELECTRONICS FACTORY, Cardiff Road, Newport. *Richard
Rogers and Partners Ltd.* 1982.
Award: Structural Steel Award 1982.
🚗 M4 junction 28 🚆 Newport 🚌 3, 15, 30 🕾 0633 52121

The eight-bay first phase of this light grey, clinically panelled factory is
dominated by the blue tubular steel roof trusses supported by tie rods from
open spine towers. The steel towers and air handling units have a nautical
feel while ducts and pipework spilling out from the roof are like the intes-
tines of a futuristic monster. Eventually the building will be expanded to include 20 bays of environmentally controlled production space.

330

331

332

333

Newport
NEWPORT COMPREHENSIVE SCHOOL, Bettws, Newport, Gwent. *Eldred Evans and David Shalev.* 1972.
Award: Forticrete Award 1979.
≋ Newport ⇐ 21 ☏ Headmaster 0633 64139

This large school complex on a confined site was planned to a rigid grid layout around rows of open courtyards. The rectangular building steps down in terraces to give classrooms courtyard views. At the lowest level, the school fronts on to a long, narrow pond. Concrete is the main material and detailing simple, but the overall effect is rather oppressive.

Rhyl
CEFNDY HOME FOR THE MENTALLY HANDICAPPED, Cefndy Road, Rhyl, Clwyd. *Bowen Dann Davies Partnership.* 1975.
Awards: RIBA Award 1976; Royal National Eisteddfod Gold Medal 1977.
≋ Rhyl ☏ Warden 0745 54980

This 24-person hostel achieves a domestic non-institutional character. The accommodation is divided into three single-storey and two-storey house units grouped around small garden courts. Each house has a pair of bedroom wings for four people linked to a living/dining area. A common lounge, recreation room and kitchen are set between the houses and the warden's quarters. Familiar domestic materials are used throughout.

Swansea
TELEPHONE EXCHANGE EXTENSION, The Strand, Swansea. *Alex Gordon Partnership.* 1970.
≋ Swansea.

This 12-storey block has redeemed the otherwise undistinguished post-war development of Swansea. Basically a large box containing sophisticated apparatus and limited staff accommodation, the exchange has little functional significance for the city centre. But as a piece of urban sculpture, it is a considerable asset. The main block has double skinned glass cladding, while the service towers to the side have ribbed concrete cladding.

334

335

336

SELECT BIBLIOGRAPHY

Architectural Design, *British Architecture*, London: Academy Editions, 1982.

Dannat, Trevor, *Modern Architecture in Britain*, London: Batsford, 1959.

Esher, Lionel Brett, *A Broken Wave: the Rebuilding of England, 1940–1980*, London: Allen Lane, 1981.

Jackson, Anthony, *The Politics of Architecture: A History of Modern Architecture in Britain*, London: Architectural Press, 1970.

Landau, Royston, *New Directions in British Architecture*, London: Studio Vista, 1968.

Lyall, Sutherland, *The State of British Architecture*, London: Architectural Press, 1980.

Maxwell, Robert, *New British Architecture*, London: Thames and Hudson, 1972.

McKean, Charles, *Architectural Guide to Cambridge and East Anglia Since 1920*, London: RIBA Publications, 1982.

Pevsner, Sir Nikolaus, *Buildings of England*, Harmondsworth: Penguin revised editions in progress.

Reed, David and Opher, Philip, *New Architecture in Oxford*, Headington: Department of Urban Design, Oxford Polytechnic, 1977.

Webb, Michael, *Architecture in Britain Today*, Feltham: Hamlyn, 1969.

INDEX OF BUILDING TYPES (BY ENTRY NUMBER)

HD